Letters from the Lakes

LITTLE LANGDALE

Among other Lakeland books by the same author...
MEN OF LAKELAND
WILD CUMBRIA
LAKELAND BIRDS (with Bill Robson)
LAKELAND MAMMALS (with Peter Delap)
LAKELAND LAUGHTER
THE LOST VILLAGE OF MARDALE
BEATRIX POTTER REMEMBERED
AFTER YOU, MR WAINWRIGHT
CHANGING LAKELAND
GRASMERE AND THE WORDSWORTHS
WORDSWORTH'S LAKE DISTRICT (anthology)
A WALKER'S GUIDE TO CENTRAL LAKELAND

LETTERS FROM THE LAKES

W R MITCHELL

FOREWORD BY HUNTER DAVIES

ENNERDALE WATER

CASTLEBERG
1995

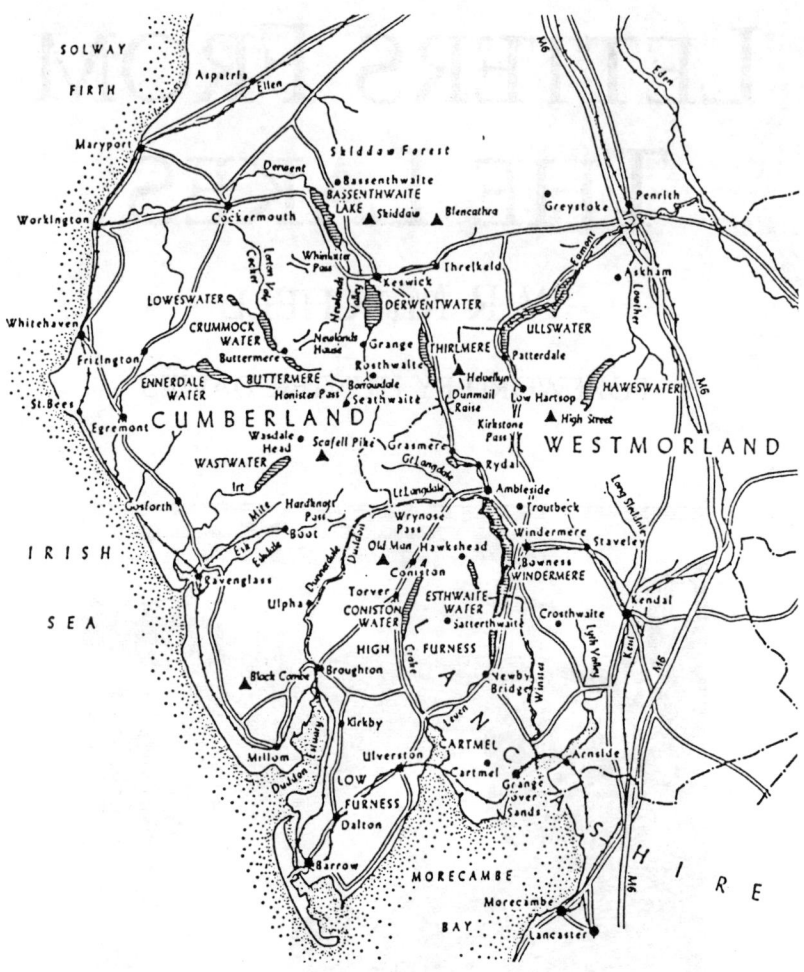

A **Castleberg** Book.

First published in the United Kingdom in 1995.

Copyright © W R Mitchell 1995.

The moral right of the author has been asserted.

ISBN 1 871064 94 5

Typeset in Palacio, printed and bound in the United Kingdom by
Lamberts Printers, Station Road, Settle, North Yorkshire, BD24 9AA.

Published by Castleberg, 18 Yealand Avenue, Giggleswick, Settle,
North Yorkshire, BD24 0AY.

Contents

FOREWORD by Hunter Davies	7
INTRODUCTION	9
SPRING	13
Mr Wordsworth's Daffodils	15
Quoth the Raven	20
The Reek of Whisky	24
Black Sail Hostel	29
Clara Boyle of Ambleside	32
The Elusive Char	35
Jim Ellwood's Geese	40
Norman Nicholson	43
Elgar's Lost Overture	47
Bitterns and Otters	51
Honister Slate	56
SUMMER	61
Wasdale Walls	63
Schneider and the "Esperance"	67
Looking for Bears	72
A Dungeon in Langdale	76
Artist on the Crags	80
Miss Martineau's Guide	84
Beatrix Potter's Shepherds	89
Back o' Skiddaw	94
Mr Collingwood, I Presume	99

AUTUMN 103

- Hotpot and Herdwicks — 105
- These Terrible Knitters — 110
- The Photographers — 113
- Red Deer Roaring — 121
- Herries Country — 126
- Sphinx Rock and Napes Needle — 132
- Borrowdale Oakwoods — 136
- Wasdale Show — 139
- White for Remembrance — 144

WINTER 147

- Swan Lake — 149
- An Aircraft on Helvellyn — 153
- Felltop Ponies — 156
- Ike's Kingdom — 160
- Coniston's Hollow Hills — 164
- Wainwright's Last Resting-place — 169

The art work first appeared in *Cumbria* magazine of the Dalesman Publishing Company.

THE ILLUSTRATIONS

Front cover: Haymakers. The backdrop is Fairfield (E Jeffrey)
Back cover: Bridges at Ambleside (F S Sanderson)
Other illustrations by E Jeffrey and F S Sanderson

Foreword

by Hunter Davies

BILL MITCHELL has been a part of Cumbria's Literary Landscape these last fifty years, a constant element, known to all local pen-pushers and most Lakeland lovers. Not quite as poetic as Wordsworth, but then who is, or as artistic as Beatrix Potter, nor as entertaining as Ransome, or as innovative as the Blessed Wainwright, but as I look along my Lakeland shelves, and I have acres of them, it's hard to think of any living person who has been responsible for more solid, sensible printed words on Lakeland than W R Mitchell.

His name is known to people in the region, but not much outside, never having had a national outlet like, say, Harry Griffin, another great outputter of Lakeland prose who has had the advantage of a column in *The Guardian*. Bill Mitchell edited *Cumbria* magazine from 1951 until 1988, during which time the circulation rose from a few hundred to 16,000 copies. His name and his writings have been enjoyed by Lakeland lovers everywhere. He has also been responsible for many books, almost all of them modest in size and specialist in scope, but most of them about Cumbria—hurrah!

I met him first about 20 years ago, when he came to visit me at John Peel Farm, the home we then had near Caldbeck. I suspect it was the cottage's connotations which interested him as much as anything. He has always been fascinated by Cumbrian legends, however fleeting or local, and knows a great deal about them. He's also been willing to share his knowledge with other writers, professional and amateur, who have wandered on to his patch, which is not always the case. Many experts can be highly protective of their knowledge and contacts.

He has written this book, LETTERS FROM THE LAKES, after a serious operation, from which happily he has fully recovered, to produce these latest musings in a relaxed and reflective mood—or so he says. It seems to be he has *always* been in a gentle and reflective mood. Always kind, always caring, never smart, never clever-clogs, never flash, never hurtful, always as interested in the past as in the present and in ordinary country life rather than the fleeting or the fashionable.

Such people have always existed in Lakeland, doing their bit to preserve and remind us of our local heritage. The best example, nudging into my mind, is of Canon Rawnsley, the Keswick vicar and Lakeland activist, who went on to do great things for the nation by co-founding The National Trust. Bill Mitchell has followed some of Rawnsley's examples, in a quiet modest way, collecting folk memories and recording characters who might otherwise be forgotten. Let's hope there will be people in the next generation who care as much about Lakeland.

Loweswater, 1995.

Introduction

THE THEME of this book took shape in my mind as I walked across the Lake District, using Mr Wainwright's Coast-to-Coast route. I strode from west to east, to take advantage of the prevailing wind. No one had told the wind, which blew strongly from the east. Rarely have I seen the district so bright and clear. Even the tarn on Haystacks, beside which the ashes of Wainwright were scattered, was flecked with silvery light. On the master fellwalker's last-but-one visit, the sky had wept.

The walk by Ennerdale Lake was punctuated by cuckoo calls. In Borrowdale, herdwick yows were attending to tiny black lambs. I blundered across the fells north of Grasmere, sploshed through peat near Grizedale Tarn, reached the highest (and draughtiest) point of the walk at Kidsty Pike (2,500 ft) and strode out of the Lake District proper on the eerie moorland of the Shap plateau.

The Coast-to-Coasters I met were as characterful as Chaucer's pilgrims. A Sussex man who allowed me to "video" his blisters recommended a special dressing—Germaline and lamb's wool. I was introduced to a dog which wore panniers, containing all the food it would need for a week on the trail. The shopkeeper at Ennerdale Bridge, who caters for some 4,000 Coast-to-Coasters a year, told me of surplus items of clothing and equipment which were posted home by overloaded walkers heading for Robin Hood's Bay.

I stayed with a couple in Borrowdale who had just been scuba-diving in Cuba and was introduced to a parrot which commutes between their home and the local inn. A visiting geologist filled me with awe as he spoke at the breakfast table (between mouthfuls of toast and marmalade) of conditions four hundred and seventy million years ago, when what is now Lakeland abutted the Iapetus Ocean. The continent over-rode an oceanic crust and the heat generated magma, which rose through and above the continental crust as the Borrowdale Volcano, the source of what is now the grandest of our Lakeland scenery. My next contact was a farmer in the yard of a Patterdale farm who was using a mobile phone and told me that Lakeland fox-hunters communicate with each other using CB radio instead of the traditional form of felltop communication—a lusty halloa, of the type which "awakened the dead".

While walking against the grain of Lakeland, solitary but never lonely, sifting through the memories of people and places experienced over fifty, eventful Lakeland years, I determined to write about topics which by themselves are of little consequence but, collectively, represent the best of Lakeland. I would do so in a relaxed, at times gossipy style, as though I was writing letters to the Reader.

On my first Lakeland expedition, in the 1940s, I was on foot, heading away from a Scout camp at Witherslack in the company of another freckle-faced, short-trousered member of what my father insisted on calling the Boy Sprouts. Two of us, keen to win an award called First Class Journey, headed for the ferry embarkation point just south of Bowness. We carried oddments of food and a couple of waterproof capes which would deflect the rain as we slept. It was wartime. Short Brothers were building Sunderland Flying Boats on a site where now stands the Lakes School.

As we crossed Windermere by ferry (a grumpy little ferry, with a slight list on the boiler side and a habit of showering passengers with soot) a flying boat, the largest flying object imaginable, lumbered into the air, its four engines rousing all the local echoes. Many years later, when editing *Cumbria* magazine, I chatted with a member of the Pattinson family whose father, a friend of the Short family, had been invited to fly on an inaugural trip. Given a choice of direction, he mentioned an area where he had some property. That day, the hens in Great Langdale would have been put "off the lay" by the monster aircraft.

As Editor of *Cumbria* magazine, in the days when Lakeland was populated by old-established farming families, and when it had the delicate quality we call charm, I studied unfamiliar aspects of Lakeland. I was never a Hunt supporter—though the huntsman was then one of the folk heroes—but I became fascinated by the ballad about John Peel. Andrew Seivewright, the organist at Carlisle Cathedral, helped me with an inquiry into the origins and development of a song which went round the world with Cumbrian emigrants and the Border Regiment.

It was through Herbert Fooks and Peter Delap that I began to keep unsociable hours and tuned in to Lakeland's wildlife, especially deer, observed on the scrubland of the Rusland Valley, the flanks of Grizedale (where much of the forest was as yet only a stubble of sitka spruce) and on the breezy ridges around Martindale. There were unexpected surprises in my quest for our Lakeland heritage. A telephone call from South Lakeland led me to an old farmhouse which had been the home of the daughter of Charles William Buck. He had been a friend, for fifty years, of the composer Edward Elgar. In an oak case, originally made for a clock, was a mass of sheet music, including the manuscripts of early works by Elgar, which (with the owner's permission) I donated to the Elgar Birthplace Museum near Worcester. That farm also proved to be a repository of dozens of Elgarian letters, some with Lakeland references. It fascinated me to chat with people who had known the celebrities. Long before the onset of Beatrix Pottermania, I recorded clear, unromantic memories of Beatrix under her married name, Mrs William Heelis.

Down the years, I have enjoyed the company (and hospitality, with innumerable cups of tea) of folk at the "grass roots" of local life. They were living their busy lives against a backdrop of England's most astonishing landscape and over a spell of a few years I explored it by ticking off the 214 fells which have become known as "Wainwrights". To those who follow the Coast to Coast path, from west to east, across the grain of the landscape, Lakeland proves to be quite small. The diameter is about thirty miles. A fit person like Joss Naylor, of Wasdale, might trot from one side of Lakeland to the other in a day.

I took a little longer than that...

STONETHWAITE

Spring

Small clouds are sailing,
  Blue sky prevailing;
The rain is over and gone!

William Wordsworth.

I heard the wheat-ear singing in the dale,
  I saw the ouzel curtsey to the sun,
    And cried, "The days of winter sure are done".

H D Rawnsley.

IT IS NOT wise to rely on the weather for long in early April. In one day, you may be dazzled by sunshine and half-blinded by stinging rain or hail. Some of the older Lakeland farmers call them lamb-storms. They sweep through the upper dales at a time when lambs are taking their first weak strides in the fields, making the little creatures wish they had never been born. In a dry lambing time, the herdwick or Swaledale ewes do not require much oversight. It's a combination of cold and wet which chills the lambs. The old-time shepherd used to cat-nap on the sofa and go out and about with a storm lantern during the night. Any weak or ailing lambs were taken under cover. It was not unknown for a lamb to be slipped into the oven for a few minutes. Nowadays, the drying process is done swiftly, using a hair-drier!

Mr Wordsworth's Daffodils

THE DAFFODILS first "danced" for Dorothy Wordsworth. I refer to THE daffodils—the golden host which Dorothy's brother, William, saw "beside the lake, beneath the trees, fluttering and dancing in the breeze". It was on April 15, 1802 that they beheld the daffodils while walking beside Ullswater. Dorothy confided in her *Journal:* "When we were in the woods beyond Gowbarrow Point we saw a few daffodils close to the waterside". William Wordsworth transformed the prose into splendid verse which begins: "I wandered lonely as a cloud".

He wasn't lonely, of course, for he was in the company of Dorothy. And, come to think of it, there is no such thing as a lonely cloud in a showery area like Lakeland. There cannot have been many daffodils in Lakeland early last century or the Wordsworths would not have become so excited about those seen at Ullswaterside. Now there are millions of "dancing" daffs. I make a special point in late March or early April of motoring along the Golden Mile, which in this case is not at Blackpool but between the northern end of the Kendal by-pass and the village of Crook where a breeze ruffles a myriad daffodils.

A retired mathematician might set him/herself the task of computing how much of the land surface of Lakeland is occupied by daffodils. It must be at least one per cent. In April, vast numbers of golden blooms trumpet the arrival of springtime. There may not be gold in "them thar hills", but gold (nothing so common as yellow) gleams back at the April sunshine. Florists and marketers display daffodils by the bucketful. Lakesides, roadsides, approaches to villages, gardens and municipal parks—all are rimmed by daffodils, standing smartly to attention until a spiteful April gale teaches them that vanity does not pay.

Wordsworthians recite *The Daffodils* without recourse to the book, beginning (as everyone who has been within two hundred miles of the Lake District will know):

> I wandered lonely as a cloud
>   That floats on high o'er vales and hills,
> When all at once I saw a crowd,
>   A host, of golden daffodils;
> Beside the lake, beneath the trees,
> Fluttering and dancing in the breeze.

The original version of the famous poem included the word "dancing" twice. The "dancing daffodils" became, in the final version, "golden daffodils". Wordsworth, like some latter-day Moses, controlled the waters. Dorothy confided to her *Journal:* "The Bays were stormy, and we heard the waves at different distances and in the middle of the water like the sea." William, who wrote the first version of the poem two years later, and had it published four years after the event described, quelled the storm but left a breeze.

> Continuous as the stars that shine
>   And twinkle on the milky way,
> They stretched in never-ending line
>   Along the margin of a bay:
> Ten thousand saw I at a glance,
> Tossing their heads in sprightly dance.

This verse was added between the publication of the first version in 1807 (when it formed part of a collection entitled *Moods of My Own Mind*) and the final version of 1815. William was not writing a school textbook. What matter if he exaggerated a little when he claimed to have seen "a host of dancing daffodils" and, two lines later, to have observed "Ten thousand dancing in the breeze"? He compared the daffodil throng with "the stars that shine/And twinkle on the milky way..." In his day, the concept of the Milky Way would be novel. In the third verse of the final version, William exchanged the word "laughing" with the archaic "jocund":

> *The waves beside them danced; but they*
>   *Out-did the sparkling waves in glee:*
> *A poet could not but be gay,*
>   *In such a jocund company:*
> *I gazed—and gazed—but little thought*
>   *What wealth the show to me had brought.*

Phrases from *The Daffodils* are now so familiar they they have seeped into advertising. A curator of the Wordsworth Museum at Grasmere, emerging from Euston Station to join the multitudes on the hot pavements of London, saw a poster extolling the virtues of a holiday in Lakeland. The slogan was—"Wander lonely as a cloud..." He doubted if anyone could have such solitude in the middle of the Grasmere season but was fascinated by the occurence of phrases from *Daffodils* in contemporary writing. Such phrases are "popping up all over the place." A journalist in *The Guardian* had described the venue of nuclear arms talks, being held in Geneva, as "beside the lake, beneath the trees."

Wordsworth was not content merely to write about daffodils; he planted them, adorning the tract of hillside land at Rydal he had bought for his daughter Dora, after whom the field was named. At Dove Cottage, Grasmere, the principal shrine of Wordsworth, or at Rydal Mount, where he spent most of his life, creating a garden in the capacious grounds, daffodils greet the spring and have been known to bloom on William's birthday (April 7). He saw the host of daffodils by Ullswater on April 15. The "fluttering and dancing season" is usually towards the end of the month.

Daffodils are now available in endless variety, some with crimped petals and stems as sturdy as sticks of celery. The

Wordsworthian Daff is the small, wild variety *(Narcissus pseudo narcissus)*, usually a woodlander, bursting into golden bloom from the leaf-litter and flowering in a hurry before the wood puts up its light-trapping screen of leaves. A shaft of April sunshine, which is as searching as a theatrical arc-light, picks out the wild daffodil against the browns and sepias of last year's litter.

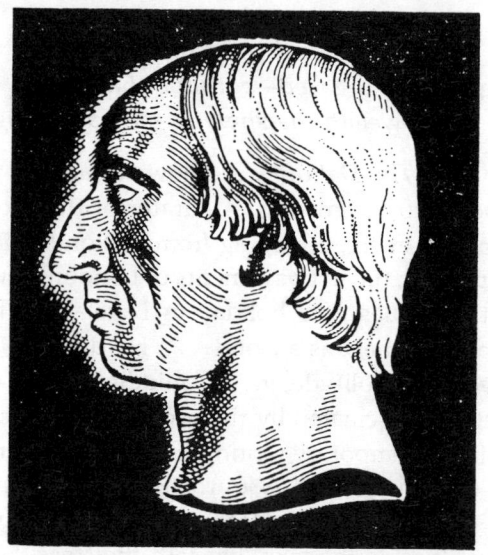

WILLIAM WORDSWORTH

In Dora's Field, Rydal, which has a special Wordsworthian association, daffodils jostle with narcissi. In some years, athletic and ever-hungry fell sheep gain admission and reduce the golden host to stubble. Wordsworth bought the field in 1826 for his beloved daughter Dora. When she died prematurely, three years before Wordsworth, the field became her memorial. It was given to The National Trust in 1935 by Wordsworth's grandson.

Lord Lonsdale, the celebrated Yellow Earl, was "partial" to daffodils and instructed his gardener at Lowther Castle, near Penrith, to prolong the daffodil-flowering season by "bringing on" early blooms and retarding others—a torment to the head gardener, Mr Jefferies, who was allergic to daffodil pollen. Each springtime, his wife had to rub "gentian violet" on his body. She moaned about the way this stained the bed sheets. When the Yellow Earl died, his grave was lined with—daffodils.

Wordworth's poem about daffodils, one of the best-known poems in the English language, had its critics. Anna Seward, writing to Sir Walter Scott, stripped the last poignant verse—a verse which was in part inspired by Mary, Wordsworth's wife—of its "truths of the imagination" by treating it matter-of-factly, observing: "Surely Wordsworth must be as mad as was ever the poet Lee...Surely, if his worst foe had chosen to caricature this too egotistic manufacturer of metaphysic importance upon trivial themes, he could not have done it more effectively."

The last verse of the daffodil poem should be played to organ accompaniment:

> *For oft, when on my couch I lie*
> *In vacant or in pensive mood,*
> *They flash upon that inward eye*
> *Which is the bliss of solitude;*
> *And then my heart with pleasure fills,*
> *And dances with the daffodils.*

Quoth the Raven

HEARING a raven's husky flight call, *pruk, pruk,* I located Lakeland's bird-of-the-mist, which plays hide and seek with fell-walkers. The raven was being kept buoyant, without the effort of wing-flapping, by a upwelling of air against a line of crags. A large bird, with a plumage of undertaker-black, the bird croaked again, then flipped on to its back and flew upside down, as though through the sheer joy of living.

I had walked up Greenburn Valley from Grasmere and was now making a back-door approach to Helm Crag. The raven held me in a chilling gaze before losing height and going from my ken by the simple expedient of half-closing its wings. The raven is in permanent residence of the craggy heart of Lakeland. Littered about the fells are the decomposing carcasses of sheep that have died from one of the multitude of quaintly-named diseases which afflict the flocks even in this age of veterinary marvels.

The raven, a sacred bird to the Norsefolk, gave its name to some of the Lakeland crags, the most famous being near the outflow of Thirlmere. The bird had, by the eighteenth century, become lumped with eagles and foxes as "vermin". The Churchwardens of various Lakeland parishes paid for any ravens destroyed. At Crosthwaite, in 1713, Widow Harris's sons killed three young ravens and were given the sum of one shilling. John Birkett, producing an old eagle, two old ravens and a young raven, received 1s.10d. In 1765, the Churchwarden's accounts included a payment of 24s.8d to "sundry persons" for foxes, eagles and ravens."

Finding a raven nest is not too difficult. It is large and twiggy, straddling a ledge high on some jutting cliff. Nest-building may be in progress in February. When Wordsworth was a schoolboy at Hawkshead, from 1779 to 1887, "bunches" of unfledged ravens were being suspended at Hawkshead churchyard and "a reward of so much a head was given to the adventurous destroyer". The records of Hawkshead bear out the Poet's recollection, the largest number of ravens produced being eighteen, in the year 1769, and the bounty paid being six shillings.

Wordsworth found the effort of seeking them out was exhilarating:

> *Oh! when I have hung*
> *Above the raven's nest by knots of grass*
> *and half inch fissures in the slippery rock,*
> *But ill-sustained, and almost (so it seemed)*
> *Suspended by the blast that blew amain,*
> *Shouldering the naked crag.*

I know exactly how he felt, having slithered to a cliff edge to peer over and down to see a nest packed with young birds. I recall the wind on my face, the gleam of silver on the glossy black plumage of a raven cruising by and the deep, dry croak as the bird registered its protest. Wordsworth watched ravens with an ornithologist's insight. In November, 1805, he saw a raven "not hovering like a kite, for that is not the habit of the bird; but passing onward with a straight-forward perseverence and timing the motion of its wings to its own croaking." He noted the "iron tone" of the bird's voice, "which strikes upon the ear at all times as the most dolorous from its regularity."

An April dawn is a good time to watch ravens for there is brisk activity as the birds gather food after fasting for some nine hours. Ernest Blezard, of Carlisle—an authority on Lakeland ravens—used to search among the boulders at the base of crags on which ravens had roosted. He was seeking ejected pellets—bundles of indigestible remains of the last meals. The pellet of a Lakeland raven might contain beetle cases, sheep wool, tufts of grass and bits of coarse grit.

Ravens are faithful to a number of nesting sites. The twigs composing a nest have been plucked from fellside trees—from thorn and rowan. Heather is added and the nest is usually upholstered with a layer of wool. The nesting season begins early (nestlings are usually clamouring for food when the dalehead lambing season is under way). During a snowbound February, I found the female raven squatting on a nest. It was the only dark patch on a hill that otherwise was sparklingly white. The raven, emboldened by the cruel weather and the necessity to keep the eggs warm, stayed.

On my last visit to a raven nest, before a permit was needed for nest-watching, it was sunny, but the sunlight, filtered by mist, gave an illusion of warmth where warmth was absent. A chill wind blew steadily from the north-east, as it had done for days, emanating from a high pressure system centred on the North Sea. As I began my ascent of a gully, the flight notes of a raven descended from a bird which regarded me gravely while gliding by. A raven is a big bird—two feet or more from the tip of its back beak to the end of its graduated black tail—and in flight the wingtips curve upwards a little. The ends of the primary feathers are distinct, like dark fingers clutching the air.

The raven's mate appeared. The restless birds called; they alighted; they took fretfully to the air and in their agitated flight made subtle alterations to their trim, thus harnessing the power of uprushing air. I stood on the cliff-edge, with that same wind lifting the neb of my cap. A raven alighted on a patch of coarse grass. The bird hopped, walked a pace or two, and stood with the sunlight bringing silvery highlights to its plumage.

The raven opened its wings and was carried aloft by the breeze. Its legs remained dangling, helping the bird to maintain its balance in the turbulence. When the wings were closed, the raven dived with something of the verve of a "stooping" peregrine. The wings were opened, acting like a parachute, arresting its downward progress, or sweeping it aloft, where twice, in quick succession, it flicked on to its back, as though for the sheer joy of being alive.

Four or five young ravens, as yet unfeathered, packed the nest to the rim. The tips of developing wing feathers protruded from quills which were arranged side-by-side, like curlers on a woman's head. A raven alighted on the cliff-top, peevishly tugging pieces of grass and throwing them to the wind. I moved on, for the young birds must be brooded. The ravens harried any large birds which approached the cliff, swooping on a kestrel which flicked defensively on to its back.

A peak of feeding activity took place in the late afternoon, as the prophet Elijah knew during his wilderness days. Then ravens brought him "bread and flesh in the morning, and bread and flesh in the evening, and he drank at the brook". Elijah must have been desperate for nourishment. Raven food is surely an acquired taste. The Lakeland bird tugs at the placenta of a ewe, or yanks gobbets of flesh from the corpse of a sheep, after using its pick-axe bill to break open the rib cage. Lengths of displaced intestine become wind-dried and lie about the corpse like strips of grey ribbon.

The young ravens fledged towards the end of April. They needed their plumage and the close company of other nestlings, for the easterly wind was numbing. Flurries of snow swept the fell-top. The male was not confiding; it glided and several times flicked on to its back. The Croaker was in good voice. The young birds snuggled in the deep nest and the cold wind whistled by them. They flew at about five weeks after hatching. The family group stayed together for a while.

The Lakeland population of ravens appears to be stable. In spring and autumn, some Lakeland birds move to the Pennines. A movement south brings some Cumbrian ravens into the Yorkshire Dales. In autumn and winter, raven flocks assemble. Each group consists of about a score of birds.

The Reek of Whisky

MOSES RIGG, quarryman, smuggler of wad (plumbago) and unlicensed whisky distiller, gave his Christian name to a Trod, also referred to as Sled-gate, which extends from Honister beside Brandreth, around the base of Gable and on to Wasdale. It is not a particularly wide path throughout and to the Nelsons of Gatesgarth it was Slet-gate (slate path). Will Ritson, of Wasdale Head, a great one for tales, which generally had a long handle to them (he exaggerated) told a local farmer, Richard Jopson, that when he was a lad Moses, then an old man, was traversing the upland trod with a pony. He was, said Will, without any supporting evidence, the first man to bring slate to the dale.

If there *was* a Moses, and if he was typical of quarrymen at the time, he would be concerned with more than slate and would certainly not return from a job with empty panniers. Seathwaite, in Borrowdale, was the setting of a plumbago mine which was the only one in Europe to produce material of the highest grade. Consequently, it was in big demand. The mine was well guarded. Consignments of plumbago bound for London had a military escort. Yet the stuff was smuggled away from Seathwaite and fed into a "black market". Moses, as he led his pony bearing another consignment of slate to clad new buildings, would also have a bottle or two of whisky to exchange for plumbago at an arranged meeting place in Wasdale.

Some quarrymen worked in gangs. Moses appears to have been a loner. The whisky still he used may, as an old story relates, have been kept in a stone hut in the central gully of Gable Crag—a building long known as the Smuggler's Hut—

or at Dubs Quarry, Honister. Will Ritson had heard that Moses operated from Honister, using bog-water from a moss above Honister Pass. He hid bottles of whisky in the heaps of stone cleared from Wasdale Head, stones which were surplus to requirements when the walls were made. And, according to dalesfolk like the Nelsons and Robinsons, he returned to the fells with goods smuggled in to Ravenglass, including tea and foreign liquors. He was a busy man! Moses was caught now and again. The magistrates fined him and confiscated his still and, of course, they'd "give it back to him on the quiet because he made such good whisky..."

Stories about smugglers operating among the high fells of Lakeland are vague but entertaining. The most lucrative smuggling trade, early last century was moonlighting Scotch whisky directly over the Border into England. Those in the wine and spirits trade at Carlisle suffered from illegal transactions and reckoned that each week between 8,000 and 11,000 gallons were being sneaked across the border. By comparison, Moses was a small-time operator—if Moses existed in the romantic form of the story-books.

Will Ritson is the only man who claimed to have seen him, which would set Moses in the nineteenth century. But Will was a self-confessed liar. More likely Moses operated in the previous century, when there was much trade in slate between Honister and the coast at Drigg. What is now called Moses Trod was probably used by pack animals operating a delivery system which lasted until 1851. Subsequently, slate from Honister Crag was being sledded down the scree to the coach road, where larger carts could be used. Thirty years later, the dare-devil scree-runners with sledges were superseded by a tramway.

The stone hut at Dubs Quarry, 1,600 ft above sea level, is in the area where Moses Trod begins its rocky course to Wasdale Head. Most of the slate from Dubs Quarry was taken away by sled down the track to Warnscale Bottom, a track which loses 1,000 ft before reaching Gatesgarth and the Buttermere road. At Dubs Quarry stood two cottages, originally used as weekday lodgings for quarrymen and visible only from the high fells. The Dub itself is a peaty area, the beck water being well suited to whisky. The building, most recently used by a climbing club, has had its furnishings wrecked by vandals.

Another Lakeland whisky-distiller who is said to have been dealt leniently by the magistrates was Lanty Slee. That renowned Lakeland historian, W G Collingwood, mentioned "the famous Lanty Slee of Coniston, who drove a great trade in smuggled whisky of his own make in the middle of the nineteenth century." Melly Dixon, whom I met in the quarry yard at Elterwater, in Great Langdale, took a personal interest in my quest for information about Lanty because Melly's Great Aunt Mary married Adam Slee, Lanty's son. "When we were kids in this part of Lakeland, it was a big thing if you were related to the famous Lanty Slee." When he was a quarryman—and his workplace was Elterwater—Lanty helped to drive a tunnel into a big underground working.

Lanty lived in a close community of men who were small-time farmers and part-time quarrymen. Some worked on their own account, having secured rights from landowners to transport slate off the fell, which they usually did in the evening. They made a living—though not an especially good one—and found commercial outlets for what they produced. One of the hoary tales told of Lanty is that he used bladders to hold the whisky he produced. Not only were these light and adaptable, but if the Revenue men were near, the skins might be cut with a knife, destroying the evidence of distilling without a licence.

Lanty was born at Kirkby-in-Furness and died at Green Bank, Little Langdale, aged 77 years. He had ten children and not once did he boast about his smuggling achievements to them. A nephew of Lanty who was a first-rate whisky distiller emigrated to New Zealand, practised his distilling legally—and died a wealthy man. Lanty made "good stuff". He is said to have offered a drink to a local farmer who had been helpful; the farmer then set off for home, but had not gone more than a few hundred yards when he collapsed. He had to be wheeled home in a barrow—and he slept for four days. Subsequently, he could not recall any of his recent experiences.

Adam Slee used to say that he discovered more about his father from the "romancing" articles he read in newspapers and magazines than he knew at first-hand. Since the death of his father, he had visited all the caves associated with Lanty. Frank Birkett, when he was a lively seventy-nine year old, showed me a cave high on Lingmoor where, it is believed, Lanty distilled whisky. He had found the cave by accident when visiting a lost sheep and had not been back there for sixty years. We set off walking from Crossgates, climbing along a well-used path in woodland which had about it a green film as the larch trees displayed their tassels of new leaves. Stories told by Frank had soon re-populated the area with the ghosts of farmers, woodmen and quarrymen. We were on a path used by Lanty, who one night met Frank's father and offered him a swig of whisky. Birkett, snr., recalled: "It was grand stuff an' all."

Frank and I crossed the old bridleway to Little Langdale, passing the stone base of a shed which once held a diesel engine providing power for Moss Shed Quarry. Clearly visible were the tracks made by horses drawing timber from the woods. We reached the remains of little buildings at Banks Quarry which does, indeed, lie in banks against the bulk of Lingmoor. The buildings were now roofless, eyeless and lacking doors. Some structures had been no more than open sheds, used by those who "rived" and dressed the slate.

At a vantage point, Frank sat down to "hev a blaw". He also wanted to "take in" a view of what he called Gurt (Great) Langdale, adding (without a trace of morbidity) that he might not live long enough to see it all again. The dale was patchy with green where the meadows were freshening up after winter. We continued, on mossy ground, ducking under the branches of gnarled trees. A buzzard circled and mewed. There was a merry run of notes from a chaffinch perched on a juniper, a tree which Frank knew under its local name of "savin".

After sixty years, it was too much to expect Frank to find the cave immediately in a jungle of felltop boulders. It was, he recalled "just a lile wee spot" with enough room, no more, for a man to stand up. It might not be viewed from above or from below. Rounding a corner in the rock, I found it—a natural rent in the crags, some six feet high at the front, the ground of mossy rock and the roof sloping upwards. A pile of stones at the mouth resembled an ancient altar. I returned to Frank and described what I had seen. He nodded and said: "I knew it was here...We've done aw reet."

Bill Barnes took me to several quiet spots on the south-western fells where he believed distilling took place. His grandmother, who had worked at Buttermere before her marriage, and subsequently lived at Barrow-in-Furness, would sometimes torment Bill by being devious in answering when he asked where such-and-such a person had gone. Her reply would be: "Awa' milkin' t'coos in t'haystacks." Much later, when exploring the Buttermere Fells, he found the remains of a couple of stone buildings in the area around Haystacks and Brandreth and wondered if they had, indeed, been places where cows had been milked—in other words, where whisky was illegally distilled. The old name for a still was "cow and worm", the former being the kettle and the latter the coil condenser.

Types like Moses Rigg and Lanty Slee throve when there was heavy duty on Scottish whisky. I gather that one or two stills were operating in the austerity period following the 1939-45 war, but nothing of the sort happens today. But hush—what was that?

Black Sail Hostel

ENNERDALE opens its mouth to the mild sea breezes. The valley is not much above sea level, though the fells carry the winter whiteness of snow and ice for weeks on end. Near the head of the dale, where there is a Pleistocene chill for most of the time, stands Black Sail, the most isolated and excitingly situated youth hostel in England. It is also one of the most rained-on buildings in the land, presiding over an area of teeming, tippling precipitation. In the visitors' book is a drawing of an Ennerdale sheep wearing an aqualung and also a note: "Bless this hut and all who sail in her." Black Sail sleeps eighteen people. It is more like a mountain bothy than a traditional youth hostel.

It is best to visit Black Sail youth hostel on foot, with time to savour its status and setting. From a car park among trees by Ennerdale Water, I strode on a tarmac way to a cluster of buildings. What used to be two forestry cottages was converted into the main Ennerdale hostel. I continued along a forestry road to what was originally a bothy for shepherds on the vast Lowther estate. The Forestry Commission, having bought the old Gillerthwaite sheep farm, leased the Hut to the Youth Hostels' Association in 1932. Professor Trevelyan donated the money needed to convert the building, which was opened in 1933, becoming instantly popular. Black Sail is named after the pass which extends from Ennerdale to Wasdale. The hostel is small and single-storied, graded "Simple" by the YHA.

Ennerdale, a pastoral area since Norse times, was transformed when purchased by the Forestry Commission sixty years ago. They ended a 1,000 year old farming tradition and, by planting stern ranks of conifers, gave the area the

Backwoods appearance. The public outcry at such vandalism, and a subsequent enlightened attitude by the foresters towards trees in the landscape, have given Ennerdale a slightly more natural appearance. Yet I felt a sense of relief at breaking from the cover of the coniferous zone and seeing treeless Lakeland, with Pillar towering to the right. I resisted the appeal of an upswinging footpath which would have taken me, unremittingly, to the big tarn on Haystacks.

Black Sail is closed during the winter. A former warden once recalled the day when he opened the old hostel for another season. Black mould had grown everywhere. The place felt damp and chilly. There is a joy in lighting fires in cold rooms and, coaxed by heat, the new-style Black Sail quickly assumes that "lived in" feeling.

Black Sail was in full view as I crossed a bridge composed of railway sleepers. Standing at the central door of the hostel was the warden, who had arrived in early March, having a fortnight to get the place ready before the first hostellers appeared. He looked astonishingly cheerful, despite a six-days-a-week routine (the hostel is closed on a Monday night). I walked straight into the common room, which is also the dining room and an overflow dormitory in emergency. Boots lined the beams. Damp clothing was draped from a rack above the stove—the sort of rack from which Grannie dried clothes and oatcake in her little terraced house.

I saw a collection of curios—cow horn, antlers, a guitar, books and also a photograph of Harry Chapman, who was the secretary of Lakeland region of the YHA for many years. Photographic prints showed Black Sail in its original state, when it provided eating and sleeping quarters for shepherds. The warden has a tiny room, an improvement on the accommodation used by the original warden. He slept by the fire in the common room. Black Sail was extended at the back to provide a more capacious kitchen—an extension built by an international working party. The hut had its own set of crockery, with a special motif, made by a local potter. Over the years, the collection was cracked or broken. The warden's sister made some attractive cups and cereal bowls, each cup being a hosteller's delight, holding about three-quarters of a pint.

Black Sail has no telephone. The water supply comes "straight off the side of Haystacks" It is usually reliable but, said the warden, "there was a day in May when it almost dried up. It rained a couple of days afterwards and all was well." No electricity wires connect the place with the national grid. This hostel runs on propane gas. A multi-purpose stove (wood or anthracyte) heats the water, provides a background heat in the common room and enough heat to dry clothes on wet days. And how it rains! When the BBC were preparing a filmed version of Wainwright's Coast to Coast Walk, he was car-borne to Black Sail and a snatch of conversation recorded while rain fell with the intensity of a tropical downpour.

Hostellers are surprised that they can obtain a full meal at Black Sail. In order to provide this much appreciated amenity, the warden has to drive eighteen miles or so to Whitehaven or a greater distance to Keswick for supplies. He buys as much as the car will hold. Storage is a problem, for the fridge is relatively small. The warden told me he likes to introduce fresh fruit and vegetables into the evening meal. As for breakfast, it is legendary, featuring cereals or porridge, bacon, eggs, beans, tomatoes, home-made bread and jam.

Black Sail looks best in the evening light. Ennerdale faces west. Light from the setting sun brings a gleam to the lake and illuminates up the north-east of Gable Crag. The hut's setting has much to do with its charm and popularity. Almost everybody in hostelling has heard of Black Sail. One satisfied hosteller wrote in the visitors' book:

> *Why, o why, do we do it?*
> *Sit in front of the fire at Black Sail*
> *and you have the answer.*

Clara Boyle of Ambleside

SHE WAS Polish, married to Harry Boyle, who had long service as a diplomat and spent his later days at Eller How, in the heart of the Lake District. Clara, a living link with some of the pre-1914 notables, had clear memories of the area before the nation's social fabric was changed by war. Through her recollections, we returned to the days when the horse was master of the dusty road; when big Victorian houses, in their capacious grounds, were occupied by well-esteemed families. Men ruled the roost (or thought they did!) and society women, swaddled in long gowns, gossiped over afternoon tea in houses which swarmed with servants.

Clara's recollections were not just of the "nobs". She was fond of telling about Old Barham, the last Vicar of Mardale, who she saw when he was old and eccentric, bent double under a heavy load of bracken. She remembered Willie Heelis, solicitor husband of Beatrix Potter, who looked more like a farmer than a professional man and who helped his wife with the housework, even to curing the hams. Willie and Clara were in the same folk-dancing group.

On Clara's first visit to Ambleside, in 1911, Nellie Boyle, her future mother-in-law, had invited Fraeulein von Grimm to tea. She appeared to Clara "a stout, elderly lady of at least forty-five." This was the sister of the famous Grimm brothers who had given the world what Clara described as "the somewhat gruesome 'Grimm's fairy-tales'." The Fraeulein had lived in England for some twenty-five years and had a post teaching German and Greek at the Charlotte Mason College, Ambleside. It was well-known that Clara would be the future Mrs Harry Boyle, but when Nellie made some casual remark to the Fraeulein she stiffened, drew herself up—and exploded. She believed that Harry Boyle was fond of HER. Back in Germany, she had shown interest but there had been no advance from Harry.

Clara knew Violet Wordsworth, great-granddaughter of the Poet and the last of the family to live at Rydal Mount. Violet, who became Fisher-Wordsworth following her marriage, had violet-blue eyes and not only her dress, but carpets and curtains at Rydal Mount were chosen to match them. Clara recalled the autumnal day in 1919 when the funeral of Violet took place and the coffin, borne down the aisle at St Mary's Church, Ambleside, was followed by her husband—"a shrivelled, pathetic little man...crippled and dying of pernicious anaemia. I can still hear the *tap-tap* of his stick on the flags as he crept forward. Gordon Wordsworth, grandson of the Poet, who lived at The Stepping Stones, under Loughrigg, was tall and handsome, also a "ladies' man" in the old-fashioned sense, though he never married. Mrs Mair, grand-daughter of the Poet and sister of Gordon, had married an Army officer and they lived at White Moss.

Clara Boyle well recalled Frances Arnold (Aunt Fan), the spinster daughter of the famous Dr Arnold of Fox How. Visting this house with the Boyles after Church, she saw Clara, the devoted maid, and was then ushered into a room where Aunt Fan ("that dear, dried-up old lady") sat in her high-backed chair, ready to welcome the visitors. From here, the party went to Fox Ghyll, a former home of the Poet's daughter, Dora, who became Mrs Quillinan. The house was now owned by the Chandos Elletson sisters. Clara became acutely aware of her figure as luncheon at Fox How was followed by hot buttered crumpets and cake at Fox Ghyll, with the prospect of tea (home-made pasty and blackcurrant jam) at The Stepping Stones, where Agnes, the housekeeper, ruled Gordon Wordsworth with a rod of iron.

Clara had a clear memory of her first meeting with Canon Rawnsley in 1914. This celebrity, one of the founders of The

National Trust, was "a stocky little man with broad shoulders, broad face and broad, close-cropped beard". He had retired from being Vicar of Crosthwaite, near Keswick, and was now at Allan Bank, Grasmere, where he kept open house.

With Clara's death, a book was closed on a gracious period in Victorian and Edwardian Lakeland.

THE OLD MANOR HOUSE, AMBLESIDE

The Elusive Char

OF ALL the fish of Lakeland, none is bonnier than the char. It has a trout-like appearance. Colour as well as weight variations occur between the different stocks of char. At spawning time, the most handsome are those of Buttermere and Crummock Water, which are relatively small, with backs of mackerel-green and bellies that look to be on fire. (The old name for char was red-belly. Other char are tinted orange, not red). The dark back and silvery body of this elusive fish bear spots of pink, orange or white. White margins to the fins are conspicuous as the char swims in the cold, clear depths of a lake.

The char occurs in those of our lakes which have suitable spawning grounds. This is the case where becks have built up expanses of gravel. Not all of our lakes meet these requirements. The best-known char lakes are Windermere and Coniston Water. Char which live in the deeps of Ennerdale Water feature in a Lakeland natural history spectacular as they swim up the river to spawn. At Haweswater, Manchester Waterworks plugged the mouth of the dale with concrete and a famous char lake was transformed into something as choppy and chilling as a sea in captivity. Ullswater char were afflicted by the poisonous effluent from the Greenside lead mines, just as Coniston char once came under threat from the noxious water from copper mines but are now lively and numerous.

Char swim in shoals, taking most of their minute food from the lake bed but occasionally rising to the surface of the lake to take flies or plankton, which is an important food, especially to young char. The adults predate on small fish, including minnows, which at one time were used as bait by the char-fishermen. My interest in char began over forty years ago, during the first of several visits to the Freshwater Biological Association at Ferry House, on the old Lancashire shore of Windermere. I heard that this lake is not just a body of water but layers of water which in summer become green through an algal flush and which hold a good stock of char, a species of fish which (it seems) was once migratory but became landlocked at the time of the Ice Age. Char in Lakeland, and in various deep lakes in Scotland and Wales, had to adjust their life-style to their restricted haunts.

Windermere is a restless lake, with two deep basins (north and south) and relatively shallow water in between, where lie the wooded islets. In summer, the lake is warm on top and cold lower down, the meeting of the layers being known as a thermocline. The layers do not mix until autumn, when the surface water cools down. Because of its great depth, Windermere has little rooted vegetation, the important plants being planktonic. In summer the algal bloom gives the lake the greenish hue I have already mentioned. Plants die and fall to the bottom of the lake, where they decompose.

My special joy at Ferry House was to visit the room where Dr Winifred Frost gathered together details of her researches into Windermere char. She had evidence of two periods in the year when char spawned, one group at shallow places along the shore in November and December and the other at between sixty and a hundred feet below the surface in February and March. The research of Dr Frost and others continues. Now it is the Institute of Freshwater Ecology which occupies Ferry House. The interest in char quickened in the 1980s when research using echo-location indicated that the number of young char was declining. Further research associated this with the algal bloom about which I had heard all those years before. Stimulated by phosphate pollution from treated sewage, mainly from Ambleside, Bowness and Windermere, a greater quantity of tiny plant algae was dying and sinking into the depths. As it decomposed, oxygen was being stripped from the cold, clear water where char were normally to be found.

The Institute, collaborating with the National Rivers Authority and North West Water, found a solution, which was to filter the phosphates from the sewage with ferric sulphate. This has already halved the pollution. Now, the sonic pulses, which can pick up the images of small fish at depths of up to 200 ft., began to show an appreciable increase in the population of young char. The Windermere char will not go the way of those in Ullswater.

A tremour of excitement passes along the shores of Windermere in March, with the opening of the char-fishing season. Its supporters troll from rowing boats and, traditionally, use twin rods, each a fifteen-foot ash pole cut from the lakeside coppice, minus a reel but tipped with a bell. They protrude from each side of a boat like the spread wings of a gull. Each rod is equipped with an eighty-foot length of heavy line weighted by a one and a-half pound piece of lead, shaped like the keel of a boat and known as a "ploomb". From the main line, at a depth of ten feet, extends a top dropper (tail line). Droppers are then set at fifteen feet intervals down to the full eighty feet. The spinners which lure the predatory char are made of copper, brass, bronze, even gold and silver from old watchcases. It is vital for the fisherman to keep the boat moving forward while fishing otherwise the Grandmother of All Tangles results.

This old method of catching char has little effect on the overal population of this species. The first char to be landed from Windermere are usually consumed by those who catch them. Subsequently, char are offered for sale, at up to £5 a pound, traditionally by local butchers. The larger char are snapped up by the staffs of the big hotels for a discerning clientele. A char has a delicate taste, somewhere between trout and freshly-caught salmon. The flesh is orange-pink.

Our elusive char fascinated early visitors to the Lake District. Camden, in the early seventeeth century, referred to "a sort of golden alpine trout" and Defoe wrote "Char-fish". It is related that Queen Anne enjoyed a dish of Windermere char. In 1700 the Dean of Wells, William Graham, wrote to his brother, Colonel Graham, Squire of Levens: "I gave your duty to the Princess Anne and said that you would send her some Char." Clarke (1787) reported that as summer waned, huge numbers of winged ants alighted on Windermere and were fed on greedily by char. "To this food some attribute the colour of their flesh in the autumnal season."

Early tourists would have been disappointed not to have tasted char, freshly cooked or served potted or as pie, the number of char in an ordinary pie being around thirty-six, the average weight being three to the pound. In the seventeenth century, Sir Daniel Fleming of Rydal (who had the Coniston fishery) despatched char-pie by coach to Aunt Dudley in London. The cost of carriage for this relatively small pie was assessed at 2d per pound, the total being six shillings. The 4 st 5 lb char-pie intended for the Earl of Carlisle cost nine shillings for carriage between Kendal and London.

The demand for char led to higher prices being paid to the fishermen and a switch from pie to "potted char", a method of preserving fish in a more concentrated form, with the use of highly flavoured spices, which reduced the cost of carriage, gave the product a longer life—and possibly swamped the char's delicate flavour. The method of fishing, with fine-mesh netting at all times of year, was not conducive to maintaining the char stock. Clarke (1789) noted that the kind of char usually sent to London in winter was the so-called "red-bellied char", which meant fish taken at spawning time, when they were out of condition. Now and again, the Londoner was sold Ullswater trout in the guise of char. The finest char were those bought and consumed fresh from the water in summer.

By the early part of the nineteenth century, a vast number of pots of char were being produced. John Swainson of Kendal (1819) quoted 150 dozens of various sizes selling at from

2s to 5s.3d each. "The average number of char in each pot would be about six or seven." He deduced that the number of char caught in one season for potting alone was about 10,800, to which should be added those fish despatched fresh from the water to markets and also those used in local kitchens. Swainson believed the annual number supplied by the lakes was 12,000.

A char-fishing outing is marked by the splash and creak of the oars and the tinkle of the bells as fish respond to the lure of flashing spinners. Commercial netting in Windermere was stopped in 1921. Much later, the Freshwater Biological Association acquired permission to net Windermere, to thin out the population of pike, whereupon the char being caught tended to be heavier and were more numerous.

A char in the hand is a bonnie sight. A flush of crimson suffuses the silvered flanks. Various writers have observed that the char appeared to glow with an inward fire. A fisherman who gave away a fine char to a local man was thanked in these words: "Eh man, thank ee varra mich. This is the sweetest fish which ever entered man's mouth."

A PERCH, ANOTHER
WINDERMERE RESIDENT

Jim Ellwood's Geese

THE DUDDON has a bird-busy estuary. In winter, waterfowl and waders adapt themselves to the movements of a restless tide. When the birds are commuting from sandbank to salt marsh to feed, a crackle of gunfire is heard from where wildfowlers tucked themselves away and are now exacting their toll. For many years, Jim Ellwood, of Millom, was one of the marksmen.

He had bitter-sweet memories of the marshes—of a wind which put ice crystals in his bloodstream and of rain falling like the proverbial stair-rods. At such times, he envied the wild goose its impervious jacket of feathers and its downy vest. Jim rejoiced when the air was calm and still; when dawn came quietly, with a water-colourish hue of salmon pink, or when both the estuary and the sky seemed to be ablaze at sunset.

Jim Ellwood put away his gun and quietly dedicated the rest of his spare time to conservation. He did not leave WAGBI, the wildfowlers' organisation, but worked within it. Fellow members helped him to establish a reserve by the Duddon. It was approached along the drive and by the house of a retired RAF officer who had a distinctive outlook on life which led him, eventually, to declare UDI (the separation of his estate from Great Britain). For a time, when visiting Jim I half-expected to have to show my passport.

Jim got his priorities right, erecting a hut and assembling tea-making equipment. From his hut, he watched and listened. Shelduck were nesting in burrows on the wooded slopes nearby and in due season he saw mothers with downy young, striped like humbugs. Woodpeckers made the woodland ring with their laughing calls. From the marsh came the *kleep* of oystercatcher and the strident piping of redshank—so strident they might be announcing the end of the world.

Jim excavated a pond and put up an electrified fence to deter foxes. The first geese, of various breeds, were pinioned but their youngsters were able to assume their wild heritage. The highspot of Jim's year came in October, with the return of the wild geese, many of them pinkfeet and greylags from Iceland which had crossed five hundred miles of the uneasy North Atlantic for a British landfall.

Jim began to plan what everything in his sporting life appeared to be leading up to—the re-introduction of the greylag as a wild breeding species after a gap of about two centuries. What began by the Duddon led to ambitious schemes on Forestry Commission land at Grizedale. Eventually, Jim was an adviser to the Balmoral Estate. But I am racing ahead of myself. How Jim got his greylag scheme literally off the ground is a fascinating story.

The Wildfowlers' Association (WAGBI) was asked for advice on the disperal of Canada geese, which had become too numerous in the South. It was recommended instead that attention should be given to the reintroduction of the greylag at Duddon marshes, the wintering ground of several hundred geese. The numbers varied from year to year; at times the roost on the high sands contained 2,000 birds. The estuary, including the roost, was used as a bombing range during the 1939-45 war, when the RAF had an air station at Millom. The geese naturally deserted the area, and the few that returned in the winter immediately after the war came under withering fire from "marsh cowboys".

An acre of land near the estuary had been made available to the Association by a landowner who charged only a nominal rent. The reserve, used for breeding duck, was also suitable for greylags, being secluded and with a stream capable of being dammed to form a pond. How would the wildfowlers obtain live geese as a breeding nucleus? They considered rocket-netting and pinioning the captured birds, and then it was recalled that greylags breed numerously on lochs in Sutherland. Goslings were brought to Millom under licence. The twenty-six raised in 1959 were left free-winged. As geese, they came and went as they pleased, and with the next nesting season they went, some no doubt returning to northern Scotland.

The wildfowlers thought again. This time eggs rather than goslings were transported from Scotland. Fresh goose eggs would not travel, the yolk being too heavy to withstand the vibrations of a long journey. Only 3% of the eggs hatched. A Scottish gamekeeper experimented and discovered that if eggs had been incubated for about three weeks they could be safely moved. Of the goose eggs brought to Millom in 1962, 87% hatched under broody hens. Well over half the goslings developed into fully-winged birds.

It was always intended that geese should spread out and breed in the wild, and the first-known clutch to be reared was by Coniston Water. Now the greylags nest in other parts of the Lake District and, generations removed from the original stock, they are as wary and unsophisticated as the wintering greylags that have not been handled by man.

Norman Nicholson

I HAD BEEN researching Haweswater for an article. Old notebooks, old tapes and back numbers of the magazine provided so much information I scarcely needed to resort to the classic Lakeland books for ideas. Yet I could not resist turning up Norman Nicholson's observations on the lake which became a reservoir when Manchester Waterworks wanted a share of Lakeland's high rainfall. Norman did not disappoint me. He had something fresh and unstilted to write. He mentioned the loss, through reservoir work, of the intermediate land, between the old lake shore and the foot of the fell. The effect, he noted, was that of big hills standing up to their waists in cold water.

It was in the 1950s that Lakeland's current premier poet and author breezed into the office of *Cumbria* and into my life. My last chat with him was at his home, No 14 St George's Terrace, Millom, the grand title (derived from the patron of the local parish church) for a row of brick houses built in 1880 in what was then a suburb of the booming little iron town. Norman called it a "quiet a genteel suburb of three-storey houses, each with a tiny bow-shaped garden at the front." Slate for building was common but brick was a bit superior!

This being Norman, he traced the continued growth of St George Terrace, which became a shopping area, with No. 14 becoming a chemist's shop, owned by a Mr Dixon and then Mr Gregson's outfitters' shop. Just across the street were the premises of Mr Slater, another outfitter. Norman told me that his father, Joseph, who left school at fourteen years old, was apprenticed in shop work by Mr Slater at a time when four or five tailors were employed making suits. Joseph then did the unthinkable in those chancy days; he crossed the street to No.14.

Millom developed as a small Victorian town, overlooking sea and estuary and being, in turn, overlooked by Black Combe. In those days, it was a sad little place. And that last meeting with Norman had an aura of sadness, with too many reminders of illness and death. We chatted in the living room at the back of the house, not the big first-floor room which had an even stronger Victorian atmosphere and walls lined with books. Norman was superficially himself. I noted as before the high-domed forehead and the wispy, mutton-chop whiskers he cultivated in later life; but he looked haggard, after a bout of flu. His voice was the familiar husky voice of a man wracked by illness. He actually "spoke" through a series of well-controlled belches. It was in this house that he recuperated from tuberculosis, which he contracted in his teens and for which he had a spell at a sanatorium in the New Forest.

Physically, the illness sapped him of his life and prevented him from exploring his beloved Lakeland as well as he would have wished. He used to work in the mornings, starting almost immediately after breakfast, leaving the jobs of shaving, washing and dressing until the end of the morning so that he did not waste energy that might be used in writing. Mentally, he was untramelled. I used to join him in an attic bedroom where, propped up in bed, he wrote much of his perceptive prose and verse. The window was as rickety as Norman. One hot afternoon, my efforts to open it ended when I realised it was about to break away in pieces and cascade into the yard.

The room held a photograph of Yvonne, whom he married late in life and with whom he was supremely happy. Yvonne had died three years before. Her terminal illness had been protracted. A Londoner, she had arrived in Millom to teach, finding accommodation at the Vicarage. Her special talents were in speech and drama. When she took part in an advanced course for producers under Martin Browne, one of the requirements was to produce a scene from a play, there being a choice of six. Yvonne chose a scene from Norman's *The Old Man of the Mountain*. They met to discuss the play. "And that is how I got to know her," Norman remarked.

When I had my last meeting with him, our conversation began with a typical, perceptive contemplation of the fireplace—"an old-fashioned, late Victorian, imitation marble fireplace." Imitation? "It's painted slate, of course!" He described two attractively painted panels as being of "potted meat marble". The mantelpiece held a tickless clock. Norman told me he had written only two poems in the last four years. "When I go to schools—and I don't do it as often nowadays—one of the questions I always get is: how long does it take you to write a poem? When I say, 'never less than three months', there's a look of horror on their faces..." Two ex-pupils of his wife were doing many of the domestic chores but "keeping the house going and keeping myself going is almost a full-time job. I am writing very little."

Around him were the remembrances of past years, including a casket and the scroll prepared when he became a Freeman of the Borough of Copeland (and caused momentary concern when he gave the impression he thought he would no longer have to pay rates). I saw a Sheila Fell colour sketch of a ploughed field (the picture was dedicated to Norman) and a study of Millom by Jim Bilsborough, an artist living in the town who had conveyed, through his work, a sense of space.

My last Norman Nicholson memory was of a cup of tea, served at the fireside. The fire glowed. Having enjoyed "background heating" with gas for years, I had forgotten how penetrating is the heat from a coal fire until my rain-dampened trousers began to steam. The tea was China, sipped from a China cup. There was no milk, no sugar—just the true taste of tea against a glowing fire as dusk fell on this strange little town by the Duddon.

In April, 1986, Norman acknowledged the receipt of an advance copy of *Cumbria* containing the article I had written about our encounter. He noted: "I am really very pleased with it. You have written in a most kindly and understanding way and I was very touched to read the references to Yvonne. And how much you observed! I knew you had a tape recorder with you but I think you must have had a hidden cine-camera, too. If ever my house is burgled, I'll be able to use the article as evidence for the insurance." He was original to the last.

CARTMEL PRIORY

Elgar's Lost Overture

NOT A WORD could be got out of him, and then suddenly he began to write furiously. In these words did Dr Charles William Buck, of Giggleswick, describe the response of Edward Elgar to his first sight of Windermere. Elgar and Buck had become friends in 1882 when the British Medical Association met at Worcester. Elgar, virtually unknown outside his native heath, was asked to muster an orchestra for a last-night soiree. Among the people recommended was Buck, who would be travelling down from Yorkshire and was an accomplished 'cellist.

Elgar needed no second bidding to visit Buck at his home on the edge of the Limestone Country. The young musician, who was still debating with himself whether or not to take up composition seriously or to continue to regard himself as a musician, benefited from an association with Buck, a slightly older man, a good listener and one who had the medic's ability to assess a situation in a detached way. Elgar had his first view of the Lakeland fells from Giggleswick Scar. In sharp weather, the fells straddle the northern skyline like molars on a gum of green.

The two young men were high-spirited, fond of japes, those impulsive and irrational spells of behaviour. They kidnapped a local parrot and bore it off in its cage, suspended from a pole they shouldered. And they "hunted" cats on the local scars. How did the two friends travel from Giggleswick to Windermere? Presumably by rail, changing at Lancaster, disembarking from the Lancaster-Carlisle line at Oxenholme and taking a train which clattered and tooted its way to the terminal at what had been the hamlet of Birthwaite and was now the town called Windermere.

Elgar's first real view of Lakeland may have been from Orrest Head, a popular vantage point. From this eminence, Windermere is like a wide, meandering river, with wooded islets and a smooth Silurian setting, in contrast with the jagged fells of volcanic material to be seen beyond Ambleside. Elgar wrote enthusiastically what he later called his *Lakes Overture*. Having scribbled his musical appreciation of the Lakes, he told Buck he had not known before a similar sensation. He had been obliged to write! The *Lakes Overture* appears to have been worked on by Elgar when he returned from Giggleswick to Worcester, for he reported in a letter of March 8, 1885, that it was "done with—I am on the Scotish (sic) lay just now & have a big work in tow." What happened to the Lakes composition? Was it scrapped? Or re-cycled, its principal theme absorbed by the Scottish piece or even the "big work"? All trace of it has been lost.

Elgar did not forget the grandeur of Lakeland, so different from the woods and orchards of Worcestershire. On a subsequent visit, in 1911, he entrained for Penrith and travelled by horse-drawn coach to Ullswater and Patterdale, staying at the *White Lion*. In 1912, accompanied by his wife, Alice, he crossed Kirkstone Pass to Ambleside and Grasmere (where he booked accommodation for them at the *Prince of Wales Hotel*).

The outbreak of war, in 1914, had a shattering effect on Elgar. The Germans had been the first to recognise his worth as a composer. It was a German, Richter, who championed his music in England. Trying to find a little rest and peace from wartimes stresses, Edward and Alice had another holiday in Lakeland. His wife made directly for Seascale, on the coast, to visit a good friend, Alice Stuart-Wortley, who was holidaymaking there. To Alice, most towns north of Worcester were "horrid". Elgar took his usual leisurely journey from Penrith via Ullswater and Kirkstone to Grasmere. He travelled on to Coniston and entrained for Ravenglass. They explored Wasdale, saw the fan-shaped screes above Wastwater and the pyramidical form of Great Gable at the dalehead. On other days, they visited monastic remains—the ruins of Calder Abbey and the rose-red Furness Abbey in the Vale of the Deadly Nightshade on the edge of what is now the big town of Barrow.

A further wartime visit (1916) was to the Ullswater area, where they spent a few days in the company of Lalla (daughter of Edward Speyer). Alice described a voyage on the lake as "very nice", despite the arrival of a storm. She and Edward sat close together under a single umbrella as the rain fell with tropical intensity. A man who had been standing by talking to another suddenly said, putting his face close to theirs, "You are luvers still like me and my wife". Alice was "rather speechless with surprise". Edward remarked, sweetly: "I hope so." Alice concluded her note with the words: "It was quite sincere & very touching."

It was in Lakeland that I located the small batch of Elgarian scores which had been penned during visits to Giggleswick in the 1880s. Buck died in 1932, having completed a fifty year long friendship with Elgar, whose death occurred two years later. Buck's daughter, Monica, inherited Buck's property and possessions. Having lost her husband in the 1914-18 war, she married Orlando Greenwood, an artist, in 1934. They lived in London until the bombing of the 1939-45 war, when they moved to Millom, thence to a house in the Duddon Valley where I was able to chat with Monica about the old days and was shown and subsequently sat in "Elgar's Chair", given to Buck by his old friend.

Monica died and Orlando lived to celebrate his 97th birthday. I was invited back to the house, allowed to sit in a chair which Elgar had given to Buck and to have some of the old Giggleswick material. Then I was shown the case of a grandfather type clock, which had been used as a repository for music. I sifted through the scores and printed material. Some manuscripts—musical works by Elgar, bearing his signature —inscribed as of Giggleswick at dates in the 1880s.

They have been handed over to the Elgar Foundation, to be lodged in their new vaults at the Birthplace Museum near Worcester.

WASDALE HEAD

Bitterns and Otters

THE BIRD reserve at Leighton Moss, a few miles south of the Cumbrian border, consists of 200 acres of open water and whispering weed (phragmites). March and April see the area a-flutter with wings as resident birds settle down to breed, as summer visitors arrive and winter visitors wait until the impulse to migrate northwards with the spring becomes irresistible.

Of the summer visitors, the sand marten is an early bird which has been seen hawking insect food as early as February. Swallows, willow warblers, chiff-chaff, blackcap, garden warbler—these arrived in the official springtime.

For John Wilson, warden at Leighton Moss, the March-April flurry of activity is a favourite time of the year. "There's so much going on." The resident birds are beginning to nest. In the evening, John hears water rails squealing, coot "clonking" and song birds of various species rousing the echoes. A speciality is the bearded tit, which first colonised Leighton Moss in 1973, when there was just one pair. "Now there are about forty pairs," says John.

In late March, a marsh harrier—the cock bird—stirs the air on its long slender wings and tail. There is grey on the upper parts to distinguish it from the local buzzards. A pair of marsh harriers has been breeding here for seven years—the only nesting pair in the north-west of England. The birds show an inclination to arrive earlier each passing year. "The male establishes a territory. Then the female arrives. The most exciting time is when they start nest-building and displaying. The male flies high, carrying nesting material, calling to the female. They drop down to the reed beds and chase each other around..."

John, a local farmer's son who knew Leighton Moss before it received the status of a reserve, had not so far mentioned what to many is the most fascinating of the local nesting birds. In February of this year, arriving back at Leighton Moss from Africa, where he had been on a census of waterfowl, and having slept the deep sleep of the jet-lagged, he knew he was home when he awoke to a booming sound—the astonishing foghorn-like call of the bittern. There are now more bitterns here than in Norfolk, which at one time was their main stronghold.

Seen as an illustration in a book, the bittern looks big and conspicuous. As a denizen of a reed bed, it harmonises with its surroundings. This rare and curious bird stands about thirty inches in height and is a member of the heron family, having a long neck, long legs (though not quite as long as those of the heron) and a tawny-brown plumage. John says the best description of the bird was that given by a small boy who was first shown a heron, then a bittern. To him, the bittern looked like "a toasted heron".

I visited John with Nigel Holmes, of Radio Cumbria. When Nigel had quizzed him about his sojourn in Africa, we walked to one of the big hides overlooking open water and 200 acres of reed-bed which, said John, "is the largest remaining reed-bed in north-west England." A bittern boomed. You might hear a vocal bittern over three miles away in calm conditions. "It's a unique sound—the lowest sound of any British bird," said John, "and people travel great distances to hear it." The best time for booming is dawn and dusk, but bitterns start calling much earlier at Leighton Moss than they do in other parts of Britain. The first bird this year, 1995, was heard calling in the middle of January.

We had been welcomed to the reserve by a bittern. In a reception area was a representation of part of a reed-bed, occupied by a dummy bittern in its typical stance, with neck upstretched and head up. When it is not looking like burnt toast, the bittern, with vertical striations on its plumage, resembles a clump of reeds. In the big hide, another bittern fixed us with an unblinking stare from a picture on the wall. We opened one of the long windows in the hide. The sounds which reached us were of gulls. Far off, a pair of swans was feeding on water as blue as Stephen's ink, beside the massed reeds.

John said the bitterns appear to boom more at Leighton Moss than anywhere else. "I think the reason is that life is comparatively easy here. They have plenty of time to call." This is an intriguing bird. The male defends a territory but apparently does not go near the nest. The female does all the incubation and the feeding of the young. John explained that a booming bird is saying, in effect, "This is my part of the reed-bed. All male bitterns keep out. All female bitterns come in." The easiest time to see them is when the females are carrying food from the feeding area to the nest, which is a platform of reed, usually placed in a dense area of reed and quite near to willow scrub, which suggests they prefer the drier parts of the Moss. Bitterns are also seen more frequently when, with a high water level, they appear near the edge of the reed-beds.

Leighton Moss was farmland for eighty years, being kept drained by a large pump. Then, in 1917, with fuel in short supply because of the First World War, the pump was stopped and the area flooded. Gradually the reeds encroached on the shallow water. In the 1940s, the first rare breeding bird—the bittern—established itself here. Everywhere else, the bittern population has declined, whereas at Leighton it has stayed at the same level. In 1994 there were sixteen males in Britain—the census is based on males heard booming—and four, possibly five were on this reserve. "It means that a quarter of the British population is in this one isolated site." Attention is given to what scientists call the reed water interface—the edge of the beds where open water abuts the reed. "This is where the bitterns get most of their food. Leighton Moss has plenty of unpolluted water. A major reason for the decline of bittern numbers in some other areas is pollution."

Leighton Moss is probably the easiest place in England for seeing otters. The reserve organises evening otter watches on Tuesdays and Thursdays from June until August. "We have about a seventy per cent success rate. It depends partly on water conditions and the weather." Sometimes, all that is seen of an otter is a black speck on the water. On other occasions, these normally shy mammals are seen within 20 metres of the hide.

Leighton Moss probably has one male and two adult females, plus the young of the previous year. A female with well-grown young provides a group of three and John has seen five otters at one time. "More often it is one or two together. They are marvellous animals to watch. They porpoise through the water. You first see the head. That goes under. Then the back. Then the tail. When they are doing this, they are actually grubbing for eels on the bottom. If an otter does catch an eel, it lies on its back in the water. If you are close enough, as I have been on occasions, you might hear it crunch the eel as it eats it." John had been impressed at their speed in water, moving underwater for much of the time. If the conditions are calm, a line of bubbles marks where an otter is crossing the field of view. "In rough conditions, otters are quite difficult to pick out."

There had been a more-than-average number of daytime sightings this year. John was with a friend on the Causeway Bridge, where water runs under the causeway, when they saw an otter pass, swimming under the bridge. One of the helpers who was painting the inside of the hide in which we were sitting saw an otter three times, no more than 20 metres away. "I don't think he got much painting done..." The otter can breed in any month of the year but March-April is probably the peak time for young. John explained that otters do not live together as a pair. "The male comes in, has a territory, mates with the female and she then looks after the young."

The commonest large mammal on the reserve is also the largest terrestrial mammal in England. The red deer lies up in reed-beds which have become a sanctuary area. "We now have the nucleus of most of the deer population for the Arnside-Silverdale area. With disturbance in the surrounding areas by foresters, walkers and pheasant-shooters, the deer have been pushed into the reed-beds. The sighting of a red deer is almost guaranteed to evening visitors when deer watches are organised, twice a week, in the late summer. "On occasions we have seen as many as twenty deer."

The red deer emerge from the reed-beds to browse in the evening. They dine on iris as well as willow scrub. "In the early days, we cleared scrub using chemicals to inhibit the growth of willow. Now there is so much browsing pressure from the deer that they do the work for us!"

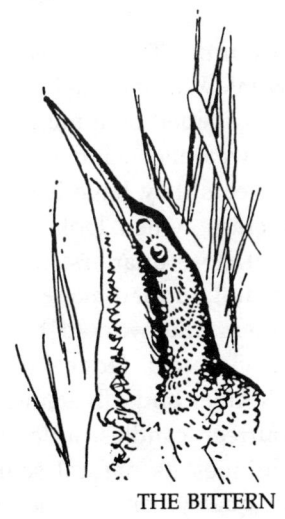

THE BITTERN

Honister Slate

RICHARD BROWNRIGG called Honister Crag the Egg Shell Mountain; it might look substantial but it's hollow. I made the short, 1 in 5 climb from Borrowdale and into view came Honister and Yew Crag (on Dale Head), quietly contemplating each other across the hause. They are old friends, their slaty sides bared with the melting of Pleistocene ice. If I had travelled from the other side, Honister would have been seen as part of Fleetwith Pike, one of the shapeliest of the Lakeland peaks, which gives Buttermere a memorable headpiece and tickles the passing clouds at 2,126 ft.

This is Volcanic Country. The fells, which are what remain of the huge Borrowdale Volcano, had a baptism of fire, set in terror and have been shaped by a million years of glacial action and subsequent weather—wind and rain, frost and thaw. For three hundred years they have been cut about by quarrymen. Hills and crags which look so substantial from a distance are seen, at close quarters, to have inclines in improbable places, leading to man-made caves, in which quarrymen became miners and worked by the light of tallow candles stuck with clay to a ledge on the rock wall. The candles, made at Kendal and Ulverston, cost the men sixpence a pound (fourteen candles, a day's supply).

The weather continues its natural sculpting of the landscape. In the 1950s, quarrymen told me of a turbulence high on Honister Crag which they knew as "wind in the crack". The "crack" is the sound made by a south-westerly wind which, arriving from the direction of the deep Buttermere valley, was broken up by the fells. Two currents re-formed noisily and with such force that men and sheep and even quarry tubs set on rails have been plucked from the crag. The valley itself funnels the wind and the fury of the wind has been such that a roadman told me of having to leave the area—on hands and knees. A group of men staying at one of the little stone buildings remained indoors one day, thinking it was raining heavily. What they saw splashing against the windows was water from a local fall, much swollen by the rain.

Fells were hollowed out by unnumbered quarrymen/miners seeking slate. Though in total the slate was some 300 ft thick, the men operated in an inclined bed, some forty-five feet thick, which lay between two sills (cleavages). The art was to cut an adit (drift) to encounter the bottom sill, and then work up to the top sill. A cavern came into being with the removal of the best-quality slate. The men took care to leave a sufficient number of rock pillars to support the roof.

Out of sight are the drifts and chambers, most of them interconnecting, so that under experienced guidance, and with good lights, a person might walk into Honister high on the crag and, an hour or two later, emerge from the bottom. Such an expedition is foolhardy now. The slate workings are closed. Details of the underworld are locked in the minds of two or three old men, one of whom told me that though the entrance to a drift may be only six feet high and five feet in width, it might lead into a cavern forty feet high, sixty feet long and of immense width.

Richard Brownrigg, the fourth generation of his family to work at Honister, was employed at the Honister slate workings for over fifty years; he moved from his old home in Borrowdale to Keswick. Dick recalls when over 130 quarrmen were employed up there. By the early 1980s, the number had shrunk to a score. The inclines are partly grassed over, speckled with diminutive plants like tormentil. The ancient screes, mostly composed of waste material from the quarries, give off a tinkling sound in a high wind and slur towards the valley. (In slate production, nine tons of rock were quarried for the recovery of one ton of saleable material).

In this curious way of life, the skills of quarryman and miner were neatly combined. The slate on the outside was poor and so men had to drive into the crag. John Hind, of Rosthwaite, who became a quarryman just after the 1914-18 war and worked at Honister for half a century, remarked that this was much better slate, having had "the weight of the mountain upon it." From the heart of Honister came slate of various hues: dark green, light green, olive and "copper barred".

The quarrymen began work at 7-30. Local men, who lived in one of the adjacent dales, might have an hour's walk to where they were employed. The clothes worn by the men were as rough as their occupation. The jacket was a kytel, a short, thin coat, popular with farmers. Their "cord" trousers were wrapped round at the bottom of the legs with hessian, to reduce drag. Almost every quarryman wore clogs. Men living at a distance stayed at small slate buildings they constructed for themselves. John Hind told me: "One chap was up here for three years; he was never off t'fell. His groceries were brought up for him in the horse-drawn carts used to take the slate to Keswick station. In those three years, he earned five hundred sovereigns. Then he left, went on the spree (prolonged drinking session) and spent it all in two years."

Quarrymen formed themselves into companies (small teams), each contracting to produce slate over a period of six months. They were paid by the quarry owners at monthly intervals. The quality of the dressed slate handled had been carefully assessed. It was always fascinating to watch men docking (reducing a large piece of slate to something more manageable) and riving (using a wooden mallet and broad-bladed chisel to split a piece of slate into an appropriate thickness, such as that used for the roofs of houses). The slate was then dressed and finished, with three basic shapes.

From the payment, the company deducted the cost of

services received, such as the time taken for the blacksmith to sharpen implements, and also the cost of supplies, such as candles, fuses, black powder (gunpowder, some of which was produced at Elterwater in Great Langdale). The black powder had arrived at the slate quarries on a cart hauled by two horses, the gunpowder being packed in small barrels, each holding 28 lb. Gunpowder was stored in the powder house and issued to the men as required. A quarryman kept his supply in a locked powder box. The hole for the explosive was hand-drilled, using an iron bar with a point which was known as a "jumper". This was driven into slate by blows from a hammer. To drill a hole six feet deep was a good day's work.

The fuse had to be paid for. If men using long ladders were working high in the roof, some forty feet above the ground, they tried to avoid using a fuse which trailed to the ground. A more economic form of operation was to keep the fuse short and, with a lighted candle attached to a pole or even a fishing rod, to use the rod as a candlestick, and try to "tickle" the end of the fuse. The men tried to arrange for blasting to take place at night, to allow time for smoke to disperse.

What remained was shared out and each man might have a pittance. Payment was down to as little as 11s 6d a day when dead unproductive ground was being worked; the men had their minds on an improved situation a month later when they were working good slate. Life was mainly bed and work. A foreman at Honister who was also a member of a team was married at Borrowdale Church at noon and immediately after the ceremony he returned to Honister Crag to resume work.

Last century, before inclines were made for horse-drawn traffic, slate was being sledded down the screes to the road far below. A sled held about 5 cwt of slate. Two shafts were grasped by the operator, who then ran down the screes with the heavy sled slurring behind him. It was not entirely out of control. He could slow down the rate of descent by lowering the shafts so that the runners bit into the slope or he could increase the speed by lifting them gently. He was also able to effect gentle turns. If he was in good form, the sledder moved in a series of enormous bounds. At one time, the going rate was 1s 6d a ton. Not many trips were possible, for after the headlong rush to the valley the man had to return to the heights with his sledge, using a much longer route.

Towards the end of the quarrying on Honister, a few men working within the crag had electric lighting and bored the shotholes for slate using pneumatic drills. An air winch was available for lifting blocks of slate, most of which were now being used for tiling and for "crazy paving", there being a lively export trade to the Continent.

BUTTERMERE FROM FLEETWITH PIKE

Summer

...Skiddaw lifts his bulk of changeful hue,
Thro' lush green meads the Greta sounds and gleams,
And one fair garden calls the wanderer home.

H D Rawnsley, returning from a sojourn in Italy.

...hear the breezy sigh
Of summer quiet die
Among the noonday hills.

F W Faber.

FARM NEAR COCKERMOUTH

IN THE DAYS of big families, and when hired help was commonplace and inexpensive, many a farmhouse was a crowded place. Monday was washing day, an operation performed manually and likely to reduce the women of the house to prostration. A typical farm kitchen was slate-flagged and there might be a "prodded" hearth rug to make it more homely. The substantial fireplace, flanked by oven and boiler, served the family needs well, the fire roaring away all the year through to provide hot water and also heat for baking and cooking. The better room, or parlour, was used only "for State occasions"—weddings, funerals and the like. All the better furniture was kept here. There might also be a harmonium, which someone described as "an ill wind which nobody blows any good."

Wasdale Walls

DRYSTONE walls are not uncommon in the Lake District. They lie in futuristic shapes around the villages and pattern the fellsides. On the high tops, sheep and ramblers use the walls as bield (shelter). Many fells are wall-less and the sheep are held in their own areas by the intangible but powerful bonds of the native heaf. The herdwick drank in a love of the home acres with its mother's milk.

The pattern of drystone walls, one of the wonders of Lakeland, appeared when labour was cheap and plentiful. Until recent times, farmers had the time and patience to build and sustain this ancient form of boundary, using material they picked up for nothing. Should a wall be gapped, the stones can be re-cycled—for ever and ever. A wire fence is renewed expensively and with recourse to a dealer in the nearest town.

At Wasdale Head, drystone walls seem more numerous, more substantial, than anywhere else. The fan-shaped tract of alluvial land at the dalehead is both a landscape and a stonescape. When the land was cleared during a Second Stone Age, the dale acquired stone farmsteads, stone walls and, in due course, a stone church and inn. Man and beast crossed the beck dryshed using a single-span stone bridge, without parapets—a bridge which arches itself over the beck like a petrified rainbow.

The walls dominate a plain at the dalehead. Wordsworth compared the pattern of the Wasdale walls with "a large piece of lawless patchwork." The writer Green thought that the dalehead would be improved if the stone walls were removed and the ground more profusely planted. Mike Naylor, a Wasdale sheep farmer, wrote a poem about his native dale in which he mentioned drystone walls as creating a maze.

These are called "dry" stones because not a dab of mortar was used in their construction. Wasdale stones lost their edges by being trundled along by the heady rush of water down the becks. They are rounded and smooth, a waller's nightmare. William Monkhouse, a former waller, told me: "They could do wi' sandpapering to make 'em stick." So much rock was available that not even the greedy walls could accommodate it. Walk around Wasdale Head, and you will see that some stone enclosures were built simply to hold—stones. Wallers were anxious to get rid of them.

The breathtaking effect of the Wasdale walls is best seen from the high fells. Those who follow the girdle route on Great Gable or who reach the summit of a vantage point like Yewbarrow or Lingmell look down and (if they are lucky and Wasdale is not lagged with mist) see the Wasdale Walls in all their splendour, with sunshine and shadow to accentuate their intricate lines. A Lakeland waller told an inquirer who marvelled at his skill: "Ivvery cobble has its feeace, but it isn't any fooil can find it!"

A drystone wall is really two walls in one, each side by side, narrowing with height, bound together by through-stones and surmounted by cams, which are stones set on edge to give a wall extra durability. A drystone wall is not completely rigid. It makes subtle, imperceptible movements. Norman Nicholson, the Lakeland poet, wrote about walls that move on stone hoofs! A good wall lasts a century and more if it is well-built. The weather is a major enemy of a wall and gaps frequently appear in the thaw following a cold snap.

William Monkhouse, a former visitor to the farmhouse home of Scott Naylor, told me in his delightful Cumbrian speech: "It would be nice if one o' them auld chaps come back to tell us about t'walls." William knew the whereabouts of "lile spots where sheep can shelter...There's a big rock yonder; you can see it when you get to t'door. Eight or ten sheep can get under yon rock and they'd be as dry in a storm as if they were under cover... A lile bit further there's a nice round sheep fold. Once when we went to t'fell we found a gap in it. I said: 'Them auld chaps walled this. We mustn't let it spoil. I put t'gap up—an' I don't think there's bin a gap in that fold since.''

He took up his first job in Wasdale in 1928. During the first few winters, frost stung hard and "lumps were comin' off t'fells." Some of the old walls were gapped. A Wasdale farmer employed a man to built them up and he supplied him with stones. The farmer passed that way a few hours later and was impressed by the way the heap of stones had declined. "You've done well," he remarked. The waller sniffed, then said: "I drooned (drowned) t'lot." He had thrown the near-useless, rounded stones back into the beck! William said: "It taks a long time before you get a start building a wall. You need good foundations. There's a lot of cleanin' out to be done."

Up at Burnthwaite, I heard that the major cause of gapped walls is "wind and wet". An east wind, funnelled by the fells, descends like a demon on the head of the dale and can give a weak stretch of wall a terminal push. Visitors damage an ancient boundary by clambering over in the wrong places. Victorian climbers staying at the Wasdale Head Hotel limbered up by climbing the wall of a barn and a famous photograph taken by the Abraham Brothers of Keswick shows the wall-scalers in action. When someone tried to emulate the feat, he found it impossible, the masonry having been "pointed" in recent years. So low are many of the Wasdale walls today that athletic sheep are discouraged from jumping by a strand of barbed wire extending from post to post along the ancient boundary.

T'auld wallers would have been upset to see (as I did) a modern craftsman using breeze blocks and cement. He was not a local man. The blocks were built up to an appropriate height and the cement used to attach to them some of those troublesome rounded stones (beck bottom variety). The uniformity, and a disregard for crossing joints, gave the wall a bogus appearance.

I'm glad that William Monkhouse did not live to see this waller at work.

Schneider and the "Esperance"

HENRY WILLIAM SCHNEIDER, one of those giants of the Industrial Revolution who transformed the coastal village of Barrow into an industrial town, commuted from Belsfield, a mansion overlooking Bowness Bay. The grounds of Belsfield extended to the lake shore, where stood the Esperance Pier, named after the tycoon's steam-yacht. On a working day, Schneider would walk through the renowned gardens of Belsfield to where Windermere smacked its lips on a shingly shore. He was proceeded by his butler (who carried breakfast on a silver tray).

Crewed by two men, the *Esperance* cruised the seven miles to Lakeside in less than an hour, Schneider could watch the passage of a wooded shore and the mini-mansions of others who had done well in the industrialisation of England. In winter, the slim bows of *Esperance* cut easily through any light ice. Reaching Lakeside, Schneider was directed to his special coach on the Barrow train (he was one of the directors of the Furness Railway) and a secretary was at hand to ease the transition between country gentleman and businessman. During a course on Lakeland celebrities which I conducted at Abbot Hall, on the northern shore of Morecambe Bay, we spent a day on the Schneider commuter route, beginning with a visit to the *Esperance,* the oldest vessel on Lloyd's Register, as she fidgetted at her moorings in the Windermere Steamboat Museum.

No one in the group had heard of Schneider until I spoke about him on the evening before our tour. The Schneiders, who hailed from Switzerland, settled in England during the eighteenth century, becoming respected London merchants, with a special interest in mining, both at home and abroad.

Henry William Schneider was born in London, had the family flair for business and directed much of that energy towards seeking and exploiting a rich field of haematite ore in the Furness district, which then was a peculiarly detached part of Lancashire, lying beyond the sands of Morecambe Bay.

When Schneider visited Lakeland in 1839, he was ostensibly on holiday but did not miss any worth-while business opportunities. Mines in the Lindal area were subsequently purchased. They consumed vast sums of money and then began to make a moderate profit. Along the hedge-bordered little roads between Lindal and the coast passed horse-drawn carts laden with haematite. In summer, the dust turned the hedges red. At Bardsea, coasting ships were ready to transport the ore to South Wales for smelting. Any ore which was mined to the west of Dalton was shipped from Barrow. Schneider and his advisers were only moderately satisfied with their achievements. They were convinced that much more ore awaited discovery somewhere in the Park area near Dalton, where mineral rights were owned by the Earl of Burlington, who later became the Duke of Devonshire.

A diversion from his business activity was Schneider's marriage to Augusta Smith, the daughter of a mine-owner. After bearing him three sons, she died while she was still young. Schneider, now based in London, made periodic visits to Furness. Ten years after he first became interested in the Park area and when the royalty was about to lapse and the money allocated for the project was exhausted, a decision had to be taken about whether or not to proceed. The Earl urged Schneider to make one final effort to locate the elusive orefield. Another shaft was sunk in the final week by desperate workmen who agreed to take no pay. At 36 ft, they struck haematite. Interest in the project quickened—and the discovery turned out to be of the largest deposit of haematite in Furness.

The Burlington Pit (as it was named) made Schneider rich beyond belief. He also had power, succeeding his father as head of the firm and having a brief Parliamentary career. Barrow went into a phase of rapid growth. Schneider was one of the captains of local history. His iron and steel works flared against a backdrop of Black Combe. Schneider married for a second time in 1864, his bride being Elizabeth Turner, daughter of the Vicar of Lancaster. They moved to the palatial Conishead Priory, near Bardsea. When in 1868 the railway was extended to Lakeside, at the foot of Windermere, the tycoon was able to buy the mansion known as Belsfield. He transformed the building and its gardens. Belsfield was to be his home from 1869 until his death in 1887.

He had his steam-yacht *Esperance* constructed by T B Seath & Co of Rutherglen, near Glasgow. She sailed from the Clyde to Barrow, where railway wagons were adapted to convey her to Lakeside. So that she might have sufficient clearance in the tunnels, the double railtrack was temporarily re-laid as a single track. The *Esperance* slid gently into Windermere in March, 1870. Almost the whole village turned out to see (and admire) her as this splendid craft, 75 feet long, with a hull of high-grade iron, powered by compound engines and having twin screws (then a novelty) steamed into Bowness Bay.

The Schneider phase was to be the most elegant in the life of the steam-yacht *Esperance*. After his death, she was left high and dry in a literal sense, having been hauled out of the water south of Cockshott Point. Four years elapsed before Bruce Logan, of the *Ferry Hotel,* bought the steam-yacht and used her to ferry people and goods between the hotel and Bowness. Hotel guests sailed in her to attend church at Wray on Sunday mornings. She was popular and regained something of her lost grandeur. The engines were removed at the end of the 1914-18 war. They were, as mentioned, of a compound type, with single cylinder block and two sets of inclined pistons, forming an inverted V and with connecting rods going down to each shaft.

Esperance managed to retain her dignity, for it was then that Arthur Ransome knew her. She appeared, as a houseboat, in some of his books, notably *Swallows and Amazons*. For a time, in the 1930s, she was loaned to the Boy Scout Movement and lay moored off Blakeholme Island (which in part inspired Ransome when he created Wildcat Island for the Swallows and Amazons to use). With the outbreak of the 1939-45 war, *Esperance* was neglected and she sank in twenty feet of water.

It was George Pattinson's father who had her raised from her muddy bed. The *Esperance* had always been thought of by local people as "the old lady of the lake". The Pattinsons used their own craft and tackle to salvage the craft. When, in 1958, George Pattinson took me for a cruise in the *Esperance*, she was energised by petrol engines and was capable of attaining a speed of 12 knots.

I first saw the "old lady" of Windermere as she lay moored in Rayrigg Bay, with a foot of water under her brown-painted hull of rustless iron and her raked stem taking the spirit out of wavelets created by a gusty wind. The *Esperance* was so perfectly designed that she could be pulled quite easily from a rowing boat. Her "heart" still beat strongly, her two 4-cylinder Ford engines developing 49 h.p. Exhaust fumes were fed into the black funnel. There was also a device for producing steam so that the funnel would not simply be an ornament. It was in the foreward saloon that George Pattinson entertained me to tea when the voyage in the *Esperance* was over. Astonishingly, the interior panelling had not suffered during the years the steam-yacht was under water; it positively gleamed. Over thirty years later, our little party from Abbot Hall sat in the saloon to hear from one of the Steamboat Museum staff of Schneider's splendid boat. The Ransome link is cherished. A stuffed parrot is perched near a window in the after saloon.

Our re-enactment of the Schneider journey from Belsfield to Barrow thus began with the *Esperance* at Bowness. We walked along the fringe of tourist-busy Bowness Bay, which Ransome knew as Rio. We glimpsed Belsfield, which had been built in 1845 for the Baroness de Sternberg and, in the Schneider period, was greatly embellished. Schneider, wealthy beyond belief, was a kindly man. It was only natural of him to think of himself as being "squire" of the district, where he served as a J.P. *The Westmorland Gazette* (1874) noted: "Nothing could be finer than the prospect from the south and west on the terrace, where the eye catches a glimpse of Bowness and stretches far over the lake to the opposite shore, affording every diversity of surface, hill and hollow for which the district is famed."

The eight acres of ground were floriferous, with many 'glass houses'. Two conservatories (one of them 30 and the other 45 feet long) were built in which to grow peaches, which would not otherwise flourish, "the dull, cloudy sky, combined with the humid state of the atmosphere, preventing the necessary solidifying of the wood." The azalia-house was a span-roofed structure 54 feet by 18 feet, mainly used for growing plants for conservatory decoration.

We boarded one of the graceful lake boats and, as she left Bowness Bay, had a languid view of Belsfield, which has for long been a hotel. At Lakeside, we clambered aboard a steam-hauled train of the conserved railway which operates between here and Haverthwaite. The spirit of Henry William Schneider travelled with us.

Looking for Bears

THE GREAT Cumbrian Bear Hunt began at Pooley Bridge. I had not long been out of hospital after heart surgery. My walking friends decided on a five and a-half miles saunter. The notion of a Bear Hunt came when, by chance, I read a newspaper article about a "crusading naturalist's mission to bring back animals from the past"—in other words, to let loose on modern society creatures which had proved to be something of a pest in history. Brown bears, judging by nature films on television, are not as cuddly or lovable as they look. And as for wolves...

A brief reference to the brown bear mentioned its disappearance from England between the eighth and tenth centuries. That's all the "crusading naturalist" said about bears. They would certainly add excitement to Tourist Lakeland. I had a mental picture of a senior citizen, dashing from Grizedale Forest, with a brown bear lumbering behind. In preparation for our safari, I consulted the Rev H A Macpherson's *A Vertebrate Fauna of Lakeland* (1892). The worthy Rev wrote: "I have not detected any historical allusion to the former presence of the Brown Bear in Lakeland." He did mention that remains of this species had been found half-way up the north-west side of Arnside Knott.

Bob led our little party across Pooley Bridge, under the solemn gaze of a wild-looking beast—an Alsatian, sitting beside the driver of a small saloon car. As we quit the bridge-end car park, the Cumbrian countryside, with its exciting sounds and scents, enveloped us. We did not wear the obligatory pith helmets nor khaki shirt and shorts. We did assume the formation beloved of explorers—i.e., line ahead. Bob, Stan, Colin and myself did not intend to be surprised and mugged by a wolf—or a bear.

The Eamont, flowing cool and clear, is a little too lively for the beaver, one of the "animals from the past" mentioned by the "crusading naturalist". A fisherman by the weir, who was seeking brown trout (it being too early for sea trout and salmon) said he would not be pleased if his little river were to be clogged with timber by industrious beavers. The pond which came into view was not the work of beavers, unless one of them had mastered the art of using a JCB, for there were impressive earthworks. We came under the unblinking gaze of semi-wild birds, mallard and coot.

A mewing sound directed us first to the sky. Was there a low-flying buzzard? From high on a bank, where grew a mini-jungle of grasses, came a bedraggled cat, its tail held stiffly upwards in greeting. If this was a wild cat it was only wild because its fur had become draggled. The cat adopted us and formed the rearguard. In places, the only evidence of its existence was the when the tip of its tail showed above the vegetation. At a road, the cat followed the central white line, causing several motorists to stand on their brakes. We gained the fields and looped back to reach the road near Dalemain, the historic home of the Hasell family, who purchased it in 1679.

We had crossed a landscape where kale would have been as high as an elephant's eye—if it had not been cropped by sheep. The cat's progress through more-than-cat-high grass might be assessed by the occurrence of alarm calls from cock pheasants. This would be good country for auroch, our native wild cattle, which are said to have become extinct 3,200 years ago (who dared to be so specific?) but could surely be replaced by an ancient version of cattle, re-created from a jumble of bovine genes and adding a dash of "Chillingham".

Dalemain estate extends from the pastoral landscape near Ullswater to the high fells beyond Martindale, an area which is a resort of red deer. I inquiried about bears. Bob switched the subject back to the cat, which we were in process of losing. The smell of fried bacon hung around a cluster of caravans. A small boy shouted, jubilantly: "Hey—there's a cat!" Sensing it had a true friend, the cat went to join him. And we tip-toed away (which is not easy, if you are wearing boots). Re-introduced wolves would fare well in Dalemain Country, where a large herd of fallow deer represents food on the hoof.

We followed an estate road towards the village of Dacre and lost our jaunty manner when, having advanced on a gate, we found (on the other side) a notice "bewaring" travellers of the bull. The morning service at Dacre church had just ended. One of the churchfolk, homeward-bound to beef and Yorkshire pudding, confirmed that bears are still to be found at Dacre. He was more specific. There is a bear at each corner of the old churchyard. The thought did not seem to disturb him. I had a feeling that someone was stroking my spine with an icicle. We walked slowly into the churchyard. A rustling sound, and the sight of a heavy creature bounding away, raised our pulse rates. It was nobbut a sheep. We slipped into Dacre church and bought a copy of a short history of the place. The author, writing about the origin of the village of Dacre, pronounced it very ancient, "as is the name it bears."

Bears? Where?

In that lovely old church, we came face-to-face with strange beasts. A pre-Viking stone on a window ledge had a carving of a winged moustachio'd animal, probably a lion. Another carved stone had a panel showing a stag with antlers, with a dog-like beast leaping on to the stag's back. The author of the short history explained: "The hind and hound motif was often used to symbolise the soul pursued by the forces of evil."

Our safari was now extended to the spacious churchyard. And, verily, there were bears—four petrified bears, centuries old, smoothed by wind and weather, given a hoary, roughened appearance by an encrustation of lichen. It is theorised that the Dacre bears are a humorous rendering of an ancient legend. One bear sleeps, its head (or what remains of the head) resting on the top of a pillar. The second bear is turning its head to see what has landed on its back, either a cat or a lynx. Bear No. 3 is another portrayal of the animal, its right paw reflexed over its right shoulder, trying to dislodge the unwelcome visitor. The fourth bear has a contented appearance, having not only caught but eaten the aforementioned cat or lynx.

So we had our bear-hunt. And found bears. The enigmatic Dacre bears now stand in lichened splendour, a puzzle for visitors to consider—and remarkably good scrattin' posts for the local sheep.

A Dungeon in Langdale

I HAD KNOWN about Dungeon Gill, of course, but had not previously explored it. Now, as I negotiated the rocky rim of a pool or hung by my finger ends from friable rock, my past life flashed before me in a trice. Dungeon Gill is for the experienced scrambler or rock-climber. Let Mr and Mrs Average stay on the lower footpaths.

The Gill proper involves over 2,100 feet of ascent. All I knew about it before I set off on a sunny day was its name. On the map, and in many a book, it is rendered Dungeon Ghyll. I agree with the comparison with a dungeon but why use Ghyll instead of the good, straightforward northern GILL? Mr Wainwright, after describing Ghyll as "a poetical affectation", affirms that it is too well established now to be altered. In my edition of Wordsworth's *Guide to the Lakes*, Gill is used in the main body of the work and Dungeon-ghyll appears in the index. The Poet mentioned Dungeon Gill Force, "which cannot be found without a guide, who may be taken up at one of the Cottages at the foot of the Mountain."

I parked the car in the National Trust park near the *New Dungeon Ghyll* hotel. Two hotels with the same name are distinguished by the prefixes Old and New. Mrs Frank Birkett, who used to live at Braegarth, Elterwater, recalled for me the days, before the 1914-18 war, when both places were run by her grandparents, Joseph and Margaret Youdell. A farm was attached. They could virtually guarantee that the food they served was home-produced. As a small girl, Mrs Birkett joined the women who were peeling onions which were to be preserved. Each peeler wore a pair of spectacles. The onions were pickled and kept in large cream jars. Lemon cheese was kept in pots, the tops of which were covered with paper which had been soaked in whisky. Milk, fresh from the cow, was separated, the cream being made into butter.

Walkers and climbers have for long been in the clientele at the dalehead hostelries. Mrs Birkett showed me a menu prepared by the Fell and Rock Climbing Club when holding a Christmas Day dinner long years ago, as evidenced by the cost of accommodation and meal—six shillings a day. To the hotels came the Eskdale and Ennerdale Foxhounds, with their founder, Tommy Dobson, who is remembered by Mrs Birkett as someone who spoke to himself. "He used to chatter away; I followed him around, but I never did discover what he was talking about!" Tommy had a tame fox which he used for poaching game, especially rabbits. The well-laden coaches of "Dickie" Riggs arrived from his Windermere hotel. He was a great Liberal at a time when this Party was in the ascendancy. His photograph might be seen hanging in the homes of good Westmorland liberals, but they hurriedly took the prints down when he married a Conservative.

As I booted up, adding waterproof gaiters for effect, I saw parties setting off for the Pikes via Stickle Ghyll. I negotiated the well-sprung, anti-Herdwick sheep gates, then turned left and moved up to a stile, coming under the stare of yet more sheep, which were recumbent, engaged in that boring but necessary task of chewing their cud. The sheep gave way grudgingly. They were here by the right of 1,000 generations. I was here for a couple of hours at the most.

The Dungeon Gill Force of Wordsworth is in the opening stretch of the ravine. Had the mountain guide been any further than that? I should have followed the well-used path but wanted to feel the chill of excitement on what Mr Wainwright describes as "an adventurous route, unfrequented and pathless in the ravines, and involving some easy but steep scrambling in impressive surroundings." I was conscious of water tumbling in the damp gloom of a narrow ravine to my left. I entered the Gill proper as sunlight illuminated it like some gigantic spotlight, stripping the Gill of its shadows and myself of the feeling of terror. A grey wagtail flew off. A common wren sang in a pitch and volume which seemed too great for such a tiny bird. Dungeon Gill became an echo-chamber.

The Victorians loved waterfalls. As Norman Nicholson wrote: "Waterfalls were so obviously ornamental, so tasteful, so discreet and damp and crepuscular—the kind of small-scale, fanciful landscape they would have constructed for themselves had they been God." Norman, infected by a lung complaint, had to observe Lakeland from the roadside; he must have envied those he saw taking to the heights—or "plunging" into Dungeon Gill. As I stumbled further into Dungeon Gill, I reached an area of tumbling water, with two impressive waterfalls. One of them, at least 50 feet high, dropped into a rock pool and overflowed as white water against dark rock. In another setting, the lower fall would by itself have warranted praise. The sunlight illuminated this spectacle and created, in the spray at the base of the larger fall, a dazzling show of rainbow hues.

I reached the core of ancient snowdrifts. The stones were moss-green. The purity of the beck meant that stones on its bed had great clarity and colour. I might be viewing them through a glass-topped counter. I was now in an area of unsurmountables—as least for me—and looked around before retracing my steps. Mrs E Lynn Linton, Victorian resident of Lakeland, followed the "deep-voiced, self-contained water" to the Ghyllhead. She found herself in "the deep, clammy chamber, where the sun never shines and the free airs never enter, but where only the waters leap for ever and for ever, falling from the bright upper world of the fell top into midnight and gloom..." An old book shows a principal feature of Dungeon Ghyll is a vertical spout in the black cleft under a natural rock-bridge. The verse by Wordsworth which accompanies the picture is far from being his best work:

A DUNGEON IN LANGDALE

There is a spot which you may see,
If ever you to Langdale go;
Into a chasm, a mighty block
Hath fall'n, and made a bridge of rock;
The gulf is deep below,
And in the basin black and small,
Receives a lofty waterfall.

I have tried to forget my adventures in Dungeon Ghyll. I recall with pleasure the loud, clear voices of common wrens, infusing life into the dark and dank cleft near the head of Langdale. Mrs Lynn Linton was to recall beckside blooms, and especially the yellow stars of spring flowers such as spearwort and buttercup, so full of life and song and poetry after the gloom and mystery of the Dungeon chamber.

An Artist on the Crags

WHEN I was young, I decided not to clutter up the walls of my house with prints. I would save up until I could buy originals of favourite North Country artists. Some resolutions are made to be broken. Hanging above the main fireplace at my home is W Heaton Cooper's evening study of Wastwater, Great Gable and attendant fells. It is a reproduction—a good reproduction—and a gift from three walking companions who had seen me through the list of 214 "Wainwrights". A note on the back extends good wishes to me for climbing the fells—and to my wife for letting me!

Like much of Heaton Cooper's work, the treatment of the Wasdale subject is delicate and subtle. I flop into a chair after a busy spell—and the large picture is a balm to my riven spirits. I feel I can look right into the view, with its shadowy boulders and the double-beauty provided by Gable and its reflection in the lake. All the features are bonded by geology, by delicate hues, by the special aura of mountain country— and, this being Heaton Cooper, by a dash of spirituality.

Heaton Cooper has produced several books with a fine art content and stimulating text (though in his biography, *Mountain Painter,* he confesses to finding the medium of words a difficult one by which to express infinite feelings. "So I try to do it in paint").

He paints the Lakeland fells with all the confidence of someone who has been on them at all times of the day and seasons of the year. He has a philosophical approach to Lakeland weather, even when rainwater is pouring from a celestial hosepipe. There are no such days as good or bad; each is either wet or dry! He works hard for his pictures, and views his favourite mountains not from the floor of the dale. looking up, but from an intermediate position on the fellside.

I once met the artist at Winterseeds, to which he, his wife Ophelia Gordon Bell, and their young family moved in 1949, delighted that the front windows framed a view of Grasmere Vale. I heard from him that the name Winterseeds is Norse, relating to a high, windy dairy farm. The buildings of Norse times would be of wood. On to the ancient foundations was grafted the stone building of today. Another time, we chatted in the living room beside the Studio in Grasmere, which took shape in 1938. Once, having an appointment with Josephina Banner, the sculptress, in High Ambleside, I found to my delight she had also invited Heaton Cooper. The main topic was Beatrix Potter, whom both had known.

Heaton Cooper once told me (and subsequently readers of *Cumbria*) about his birth and early upbringing in what us now called Gatehouse at Coniston. His father, Alfred Heaton Cooper, born in 1863, was the son of a book-keeper in a Bolton cotton mill and an uneducated mill girl. He jibbed at a career in accountancy at the Town Hall and gained a scholarship to Westminster School of Art in London. Alfred's special themes in art were the interplay of light on natural scenes at specific times of day and season. He was also fascinated to see native Lakelanders at work in various rural settings.

Alfred Heaton Cooper preferred to work out-of-doors, having a special love of mountain country which led him to Scotland, Lakeland and Norway. In the last-named country he met and (in 1894) married Mathilde Marie Valentinsen. They arrived at Hawkshead, intending to make the Lake District their home, in 1898. The timber-built Norwegian building which has overlooked Lake Road, Ambleside, since 1914 was constructed in 1905 from whole pine logs which Alfred imported from Norway, the wooden building originally serving as a studio and gallery in Coniston.

Alfred struggled for recognition and to cater for a growing

family. Artistically, the breakthrough came in 1904, when A & C Blacks commissioned him to provide 75 paintings, to be reproduced in colour as illustrations in *The English Lakes,* a book being written for them by W T Palmer. The paintings would be purchased outright by the publishers for £150 and fifty pounds. In due course, Alfred contributed to thirteen of these regional topographical works which are now highly-collectable.

Alfred Heaton Cooper died in 1929. His son, William Heaton Cooper, developed his love of painting the fell country of Lakeland through seeing the Coniston Fells when he was young. He became passionate about rock-climbing. I asked him when he had taken up serious rock climbing. He replied: "I was never serious. It was always fun...I began before my tenth birthday, in the company of my brothers and sisters. I was never particularly good as a climber, but enjoyed the sport enormously."

At the age of fifteen, anxious to take up climbing, he visited Keswick for a pair of boots. They were farmer's boots, with big nails and 'caulkers'. The boots were almost as hard as wood, so he walked from Keswick to Grasmere, where he was then living, following the felltops, to ease them in. "There were a lot of bogs on the way. By the time I got to Grasmere, they were easier to wear—but I was rather tired." When he attained his majority, Heaton Cooper was still a lone climber. Two young people asked him to show them some Lakeland climbs, and he agreed. "I had heard of a crag called Gimmer but had never found it. I had never looked for it really. I hadn't a rope, so I went to a farmer friend and borrowed 40 feet of cart rope." The little party did not complete this climb. When Heaton Cooper told me of this adventure, the climb—now graded "severe"—had only just been climbed in its entirety.

Heaton Cooper drawings have been reproduced in many editions of the climbing guides. Harry Kelly had been asked to edit a new set of guides. "He wasn't satisfied with the photographic illustrations which had been used, for they did not reveal the rock in sufficient detail for a climber to follow them. A smudge on the photograph might be a juniper bush, a tuft of heather or an overhang. He asked me if I would do him some drawings..." The first feature to be so illustrated, in 1935, was Pillar Rock. "I did a lot of climbs with Kelly and Holland and others. I climbed with some of the giants of climbing and I was lucky to have their company."

So successful was this line-work that Heaton Cooper illustrated more guides. His phenomenal knowledge of Lakeland crags ensured that he made sketches at times when the features were best displayed. For example, for the guide to Scafell he found that the face is best revealed in sunlit detail between five and six in the morning and about eight in the evening during the month of June. He told me that originally the drawings were reproduced in photogravure so that a half-tone effect was achieved. The climbing routes were superimposed in ordinary letterpress and, being much darker, they stood out from the impressions of the crags.

Heaton Cooper's real love was painting, not rock climbing. "I did rock climbing for fun. It was nice to make such good friends. I'm really very sad when people take up climbing in the Lake District as seriously as they do now. Last year (1985) there were 230 first ascents. Some of them were about 40 feet, which is absolute nonsense. We would not have thought about recording a little bit of rock 40 feet high..."

It was fascinating to watch Heaton Cooper at work in his studio, where he did not have to work urgently, to record some fleeting moments in the Lakeland day. In his autobiography, he suggests that each subject must be allowed to dictate design and treatment, "so that every painting becomes a new and exciting adventure." The sort of mountain country which appealed is where he could look from a high broad ridge, containing one or more tarns, to higher mountains. An instance of this is the craggy north side of Fairfield from Angle Tarn above Patterdale.

Miss Martineau's Guide

IN THE mid-nineteenth century, a railway from Kendal arrived at the hamlet of Birthwaite, a mile or so from the eastern shore of Windermere. The railway company adopted the name of the lake for its terminus. Miss Harriet Martineau, of The Knoll, Ambleside, wrote: "A few years ago there was only one meaning to the word WINDERMERE. Now there is a Windermere Railway Station, and a Windermere post office and hotel;—a thriving village of Windermere and a populous locality."

The coming of the Iron Horse transformed life in this part of Lakeland. A new guide to the Windermere district was required. And Miss Martineau, writer, lecturer, thinker, social reformer, was just the person to provide it. She was an off-comer who, none the less, had rapidly absorbed Lakeland lore and history, who knew the Lakeland celebrities of the time, who was associated with Charlotte Mason's College and wrote furiously. She was born in Norfolk in 1802, being the daughter of a wealthy manufacturer of French descent. Miss Martineau had an awesome intellect. When she was twenty-one years old, she wrote a theological novel, followed—between 1832 and 1834—by a nine volume work, *Illustrations of Political Economy*.

Her growing reputation as a writer gave her access to the political and literary coteries of London. She was an outspoken critic of what she saw as social ills and, spending two years in the United States, she caused some turmoil by her strong views on the ills of slavery. Miss Martineau was physically weak. She had been a sickly child and bouts of ill-health were to recur through her life. Returning to England, she was seriously ill and alarmed her family by attempting to cure herself through mesmerism. It worked—up to a point. She resumed her busy round of writing, talking and travelling, this time to Palestine and Egypt. At the age of 44, Miss Martineau found a measure of peace when she settled at The Knoll, Ambleside, an area she had got to know during a holiday spent at Windermere.

She moved into her new home with two servants, oddments of furniture donated by friends, books and files. Among her new friends were the Wordsworths, who lived a short distance up the road at Rydal, and Matthew Arnold, Headmaster of Rugby, who had a house Under Loughrigg. Her principal tenets were what she saw as truth and justice. Family and friends were dismayed at her rejection of orthodox Christian beliefs, such as the notion of a personal God. Matthew Arnold told a friend he had "talked to Miss Martineau—who blasphemes frightfully."

She was disappointed by the attitudes of others, including William Wordsworth. When they met, the talk was not of Poetry or Nature but of the cash value of The Knoll. Wordsworth calculated she had done well for herself in purchasing it; the property would double in value in a decade." He chose a motto for her garden sundial—"Come, Light! Visit me!" He horrified her by suggesting she follow the Wordsworth example with a visitor of providing a cup of tea free of charge but making a charge if any meat was required. She discovered that Wordsworth was so vehement on this matter because he had about 500 casual visitors each summer.

Miss Martineau was often away from Ambleside, travelling and lecturing. Her visitors to The Knoll included George Eliot, Mrs Gaskell and Charlotte Bronte, who wrote to Ellen Nussey: "Her house is very pleasant, both within and without; arranged at all points with admirable neatness and comfort. Her visitors enjoy the most perfect liberty; what she claims for herself she allows them. I rise at my own hour, breakfast alone (she is up at five, takes a cold bath, and a walk by starlight, and has finished breakfast and got to her work by seven o' clock)."

Miss Martineau's principal discomfort was deafness. She resorted to the use of an ear trumpet. Articles by the hundred and a stream of profound books came from her pen. In 1854 her *Guide to Windermere* was published, followed in 1855 by *A Complete Guide to the English Lakes*. It is the Windermere guide which fascinates me. The district was entering its period of lusty Victorian growth. She wrote when the recent arrival of the railway was transforming life in the area. Her own house is mentioned as "the residence of Miss H Martineau". Also noted are those of her neighbours—"Tranby Lodge, the white house to the left and the abode of Alfred Barkworth, Esq.; Green Bank, the estate of Benson Harrison, Esq., and Low Nook, "the pretty cottage next reached on the same side", where lived Miss Head.

Ambleside new church did not appeal to her. She described it as "more of a blemish than an adornment, unhappily, from its size and clumsiness, and the bad taste of its architecture. Though placed in a valley, it has a spire—the appropriate form of churches in a level country; and the spire is of a different colour from the rest of the building; and the east window is remarkably ugly." At Grasmere, she mentioned "the cluster of lodging-houses, called St Oswald's, where the Hydropathic Establishment struggled on for a time, but found the Westmorland winters too long for invalids." The *Red Lion* was described as an old-fashioned little place, where "the traveller's choice is usually between ham and eggs and eggs and ham; with the addition, however, of cheese and oat cake."

To the main text of her guide-book were added details of excursions to and from Keswick and an account of the flowering plants, ferns and mosses of the district. There was also "an accurate map". The bound edition cost 10s. The cost of production was subsidised by advertisements, including one for *Ullock's Royal Hotel,* the proprietor of which, W Bownass, returned his warmest thanks to the Royal Families,

Nobility, Gentry and the public for their liberal support. *Rigg's Windermere Hotel* specialised in its transport facilities—open and close carriages, cars and post-horses. The *White Lion* at Ambleside offered a billiards room. "An omnibus daily meets the Steamers at Windermere Waterhead."

Miss Martineau's guide deals with a Lakeland newly linked by tracks of steel to the main rail network. The branch line from Kendal was having a major impact on a cluster of Lakeland settlements. Wordsworth was bitterly opposed to the railway. Harriet could deal with its arrival dispassionately, writing: "It is a great thing that steam can now convey travellers round the outskirts of the district and up to its openings." The buildings of the "new" village of Windermere were fashioned "of the dark grey stone of the region", being "for the most part of a mediaeval style of architecture. The Rev J A Addison, of Windermere warden of a college intended chiefly for the sons of clergymen, has a passion for ecclesiastical architecture; and his example has been a good deal followed..."

Villas had appeared on either side of the road, on almost every favourable spot, all the way from Windermere to Bowness, the "port of Windermere", where "the new steamboats put up and thence go forth the greater number of fishing and pleasure boats which adorn the lake." *Ullock's Hotel,* which had been called *Royal* since the visit of Queen Adelaide in 1844, now made up between seventy and eighty beds. "Close at hand is a little museum, where the birds of the district may be seen, exceedingly well stuffed and arranged by Mr Armstrong, a waiter at the hotel." The *Crown Hotel* had ten private sitting rooms and made up ninety beds. Local delicacies included fish. Coniston was noted for its potted char and "as for the trout, there can be none finer than that of Windermere."

Miss Martineau commended Ferry Nab, on the southern side of Bowness Bay, as a charming resting-place. "It is breezy here; and the waters smack the shore cheerily." The ferry-boat, heavy and roomy, propelled by men with ponderous oars, was capable of taking horse and carriage, the horse being unharnessed and led by itself on to the boat. To the north of the Bay was Rayrigg and beyond this Miller Brow, with a new house built for William Sheldon, "the most enviable abode in the country—commanding a view worthy of a mountain top, while sheltered by hill and wood, and with the main road so close at hand that the conveniences of life are as procurable as in a street."

Having made the three recommended tours, there was one thing a stranger must do before he went on into Cumberland. "He must spend a day on the Mountains; and if alone, so much the better...Let him go forth early, with a stout stick in his hand, provision for the day in his knapsack or his pocket; and, if he chooses, a book: but we do not think he will read to-day." Fairfield, Ambleside's own mountain, was recommended. "The stranger had better come on to Ambleside by the early mail, and breakfast there." We are told that an old shepherd had charge of four rain gauges, set up on four ridges—"desolate, misty spots, sometimes below and often above the clouds."

EASEDALE TARN

Beatrix Potter's Shepherds

BEATRIX POTTER'S life in Lakeland may be neatly divided into two parts. The first concerns a shy spinster, writer and artist, who made birds and animals lovable by dressing them up in clothes and who provided nursery tales for generations of children. In the second part she was Mrs Heelis, wife of a shy Lakeland solicitor who on courting nights arrived at her home in Near Sawrey by motor-bike. She was also a farmer, with more enthusiasm than detailed knowledge of livestock. In her later days, she had some sacking as a pinafore and clattered about in clogs.

Tom Storey, who worked for her as farm man and shepherd for 18 years, and served under Mr Heelis for another two, told me: "Beatrix thought a lot about the Herdwick sheep; she wasn't particularly interested in farming in general. She didn't knaw one cow from another..." Whenever I was in the Sawrey area, I'd pop in to see Tom for what Lakeland folk call a crack (gossip). He was a typical Lakeland dalesman—small, spare, quiet-spoken, with a wry humour, and though clearly respectful of his famous employer not above having a dig at her when she said or did something which in a farming sense was—daft.

"All the old sheep farmers knew her. She'd talk for a week to a real old sheep farmer. She didn't always ken (recognise) her own sheep. At Keswick, I was showing yan of t'elder sheep, a ewe. I saw Mrs Heelis and two farmers walking near the pens. They stopped suddenly. She talked about sheep. Then she whipped round and said: 'Which is such-and-such ewe, Storey, among these?' I said: 'Them aren't yours! Yours are in next pen.' Was her face red? I don't think she liked it but she daren't say anything. I was only telling the truth..."

I first met Tom Storey in 1955. He had arrived at Sawrey from Troutbeck some sixty years before. He was in farm work at Troutbeck in 1926 when she tracked him down, having had him recommended as a good man. She offered him a job at Troutbeck Park, a huge sheep farm at the head of the valley. Tom was married, with two young children, and lived in a cottage in the village. He was at Troutbeck Park for only twelve months. "It had been tupping (mating) time for the sheep when I went in November. I put rams on to a thousand breeding ewes and I lambed them the following spring."

Tom recalled that when she visited the farm, she did not often enter the house but invariably went for a walk on the fell. She would be found sitting at Tongue End when Tom returned from kenning the sheep and she wanted to know all about his trip. Mrs Heelis asked him to take over at Hill Top, Sawrey. When Tom and his family moved, they piled their belongings on the back of a motor lorry kept by Beatrix for heavy farm jobs. Sawrey was wick (lively) with Peter Rabbits. "It was terrible...Grass couldn't grow for rabbits." They were especially common on Beatrix's seventy acres of land beyond Esthwaite Water. Tom caught nine hundred rabbits in one month.

Beatrix's days as writer and artist were no means over. She gave him the first copy of her *Fairy Caravan*. Farming occupied much of her thoughts. "She didn't try to keep up with the times. We did at least have a mowing machine at haytime. She gave a hand, raking up." Beatrix told Tom of a desire to paint a lamb and asked him to let her have the head of the next lamb to die. He did so. She fastened the head against a wall and sat on a copy (stool) in a field to paint it. Tom's later years were spent in a lile cottage at the end of a row at Near Sawrey. I'd first see him through the window. He'd be sitting in a fireside chair and in an uncluttered room. He'd wave. I'd enter to a warm welcome—and often a nip o' summat strong.

She was a good employer but she could be funny. "You

could meet her one time, and she'd never look sideways at you. Another time she would stop and talk. She never liked to talk for long." Tom's duties were capable of wide interpretation. He used to row the boat when William Heelis went fishing on Moss Eccles Tarn. Beatrix had stocked the tarn with brown trout and, said Tom, "her husband *could* fish. I've seen him throw a fly a long way and he caught some fine trout. He'd give me some, but my family didn't care a big lot for them; they tasted a bit 'mossy'." Beatrix chattered now and again about things she could see up the intake. She was fascinated by sheep and lambs and wanted to know who owned which stock of sheep.

I recall with special clarity my last meeting with Tom. Arriving at his cottage home in Sawrey, I rapped my knuckles against the door and listened for his ever-bright "Come in!" This time the response was delayed. There was time to glance through the window. His favourite chair was empty. He called faintly, inviting me to enter. Tom lay in bed, suffering from an old chest complaint. A few weeks before, he had told me of his impending ninetieth birthday. I asked him about it. "It's today," he announced. We celebrated, Tom and I, with glasses of sherry. We chatted for a while until members of his family arrived with gifts and good wishes.

Anthony Benson, who was also a shepherd employed by Mrs Heelis, was living at Plumpton Foot, not far from Penrith, when I met him. He first worked at Troutbeck Park as a lad fresh from school (the farm was then owned by Mrs Leach); he then moved away and had a variety of jobs. He was working for Isaac Fleming when he heard from Mr Heelis, who was Isaac's solicitor, that a shepherd was needed at the Park. Anthony had an appointment to see Mrs Heelis.

He asked her about the wage he would receive. (He had been paid 25s a week). Mrs Heelis offered him 50s, "straight off" and also built the Bensons a cottage. "She kept us in coal. She fed five or six dogs. So that wage was as good as 60s." He was a shepherd at Troutbeck Park for 15 years. He told me, with mock gravity, that in 15 years Beatrix had not paid him once. A pause. He added: "She usually paid t'wife, saying that money should go into the home."

In Anthony's recollection, Mrs Heelis was "a lish body" who loved to visit the fields where sheep were kept or she'd set off on a hill track. Clipping time, with its noise and bustle, excited her. "We clipped between 2,000 and 3,000 sheep—all Herdwicks, though on a fell-spot like Troutbeck it wasn't always easy to keep the flock pure wi' stray tups coming in from other places." It took us seven hours just to gather the sheep, which went as far as High Street. "Then I've seen us sit down of a morning at seven o'clock and clip, then git up and have our dinners, and back and sit down again, and clip till six o'clock. It went on maybe for a fortnight or three weeks. There were always four of us clipping. We fed well..."

It was customary to hire a tup in at Keswick in autumn and return it to its owner in the spring. Then the old hiring custom began to give way to outright sales. The best tups were in keen demand and if Mrs Heelis wanted one "she would have it", paying £200 for an especially good tup. At Keswick Tup Fair, she wore the same old costume, day in and day out. "It was a thick tweed and reet doon to her ankles." Anthony confirmed what Tom had told me, that "she didn't knaw a gurt lot about sheep. She was one o' those who'd take a fancy to one sheep when there were mebbe plenty o' better 'uns." She took notice of what her friends the old Lakeland flockmasters had to say. They included Isaac Thomson, who used to be at West End, Wythburn, and Ned Nelson of Gatesgarth.

Tom Storey was with Mrs Heelis a few hours before she died in 1943. She wanted to see him. Mrs Rogerson, who looked after her, admitted him to the house. Mrs Heelis lay in bed. There was no fire in the room. "I sat down and we chatted about farming. She asked how things were going on. I think she thought she was 'going' judging by the way she talked to me that night. She asked me to carry on looking after the farm for Mrs Heelis after her day." Tom didn't stay long. Mrs Heelis died during the night.

I have already mentioned by last visit to Tom. On my next visit to Sawrey, I heard that he was dead and buried. For me, Near Sawrey had lost some of its lustre.

Back o' Skiddaw

THE BAREST, emptiest, quietest area of Lakeland lies "back o' Skiddaw". It has a grand romantic name—Skiddaw Forest—yet there is hardly a tree on it. Wainwright in his pictorial guide to the Northern Fells referred to "a vast upland basin" and as "an upland depression rimmed by summits". It was country that appealed to him. He noted, with enthusiasm: "This is a land of solitude and silence." I suspect that he thought more of sheep than people. Where the slatey Skiddaw fells, smooth and rounded, are like a petrified sea-swell, sheep by the hundred are the official green-keepers, each dividing the day into three—champing time, cud-chewing time and sleep. What do these Skiddaw sheep dream about?

Wainwright turned the hitherto obscure Pearson Dalton, the last of the shepherds, into a modern folk hero. Pearson and his dogs spent many a night at Skiddaw House, the only feature in Skiddaw Forest which smacks of humanity. At the time Wainwright produced his pictorial guide featuring Back o' Skiddaw, Pearson was well into his stride, following the Caldew westwards to its source among the peat-pots.

Skiddaw House, this strange, terrace-like building, the loneliest house in Lakeland, may be approached from at least five directions. Once, I descended to the House from the flanks of Skiddaw. Another time, I strode in from the north, using the valley of the Dash and having a butty-stop by the waterfalls. On yet another occasion, the approach was over proud Blencathra and across a depressing tract of mossland to where Skiddaw House appeared to view, looking incongruous in this huge peaty area, where foxes bark and curlews dip and call. From Mungrisedale, the path lies beside the boisterous River Caldew, a watercourse in a tousled landscape which has something of the appearance of the Scottish Highlands.

It is a relatively easy saunter from near the old sanatorium at Threkleld (a cluster of buildings now used as a youth centre). The broad path lies through a V-shaped gash between Blencathra and Lonsdale Fell, the last-named rising in a series of dizzying verticals. Skiddaw House itself is not easy to pick out at a distance. A walker aims for an adjacent plantation, which is pruned naturally by winter gales. The building, once a shepherd's abode, is now a youth hostel during what some refer to as the "warmer months". The warden usually leaves his car where the tarmac ends near Threlkeld and cycles to his remote place of work. This was the route I last used, with the track appearing to make a bee-line for Great Calva (2,265 ft), which is everyone's idea of a mountain, being shaped like a cone. The walker who does not know this area enters Skiddaw Forest with some disappointment, for this area is not a forest in the conventional sense. Perhaps it never was, being the type of early forest which was merely land set aside for hunting. Mrs E Lynn Linton, who visited this area in the 1860s, later wrote of "Skiddaw and its forest—where is never a tree, but only moor birds and ling [heather]."

The big hills which fill the skyline in every direction have a rounded, hunched appearance, as though taking a defensive attitude against the grim weather. Even in spring, sunny periods may alternate with showers of hail which periodically silver the head of Skiddaw. The path swerves, climbs and reaches operational height. It is now an easy saunter to Skiddaw House. Mrs Linton mentioned this building as "a certain shooting-box of enviable circumstance." The novelist Hugh Walpole, creator of the Herries family, had Skiddaw House in mind when he penned *The Fortress,* a building in a wild situation. In Walpole's *The Bright Pavilions,* Robin Herries attended somewhere remarkably like Skiddaw House for a secret celebration of the Mass.

The last-known shepherd to live here, the celebrated Pearson Dalton, was a power in this landscape over thirty years ago. His ghost was conjured up by a warden of the youth hostel for an imaginative visitor as he prepared to go to bed. Blood ran cold as the tale was told of a spectral Pearson Dalton, with a spectral dog, disappearing through a wall. The warden said they had returned to look at the old place. Skiddaw House became derelict until a new owner allowed it to serve as a youth hostel, from March to October.

I was at Skiddaw House twice in 1993. On the first occasion, it was locked up. A notice indicated it was open every night at 5 p.m. normally "or earlier on some days when warden is around". A bothy at the end of the row is open at all times. Inside I found a bivvy bag and a tin of soup. On my next visit, the warden, Martin Webster, recalled opening up the hostel in late March and then settling back to await the arrival of hostellers. The first of them booked in five days later.

Martin's fascination for Skiddaw House began when it was being manned by volunteers. Then the duty warden, who was a great friend, appeared at the door of the members' common room, fully dressed and with his rucksack packed. He asked Martin if he was serious about wanting to be a warden, and when Martin indicated he was, the keys were thrown to him with the words: "Look after the place. Stay here till the next volunteer comes."

At the end of his first season, Martin asked if he could stay on for an extra month, at his own expense, to do jobs like recovering floors and varnishing. If he had some spare time, he "nipped" up Skiddaw. He loved to sit on a bench in front of Skiddaw House on a summer dawn, when the cock grouse were crowing from the heathered slopes of Great Calva.

Skiddaw House has electrical power provided by four storage batteries which are charged-up using a small generator, so the use of fluorescent lights is possible. The water supply, fresh and clear, comes off Sale How Fell. Four upstairs dormitories are complete with bunks, blankets and even matching curtains. Upstairs, too, are a washroom and toilet for ladies. Downstairs is the men's sleeping accommodation and a members' dining room, with a fireplace at each end, fed by dead wood from the plantation behind the House. Hot water is on tap in the kitchen, courtesy of a gas-fired boiler.

The area around the infant Caldew is split up into five heafs for sheep. The lives of the fell families revolved around sheep, the year being punctuated by lambing, dipping, clipping, spaining (separation of ewes and lambs) and the autumn sales, followed by tupping. Harrison Wilson used to tell me of t'auld days—of shepherds' meets and the local shepherds' feast. Shepherds met at Wylie Ghyll (a convenient spot for farmers living over a wide area) on the last Monday in July. On the previous day, a barrel of beer had been taken up there on horseback. The barrel was "tapped" and then allowed to settle down overnight. The second meet, at Black Hazel, opposite the Ghyll, took place on the first Monday after the 29th October. In the colder weather, men took with them some whisky and rum.

A few stray sheep might be taken to the shepherds' feast, which was held on the first Monday in December at five places in rotation—Mungrisedale, Threlkeld, Bassenthwaite, Uldale and Caldbeck. The feast had as it main feature a tatie-pot, into which mutton, black puddings and potatoes had been dropped. "It was near Christmas, so they always had some plum pudding. It was a real good do."

Caldew's enormous catchment area is the periphery of Skiddaw Forest, a distance of some thirteen miles. Not surprisingly, the river has been known to rise and fall two feet in a day. When the Caldew overflows near Mosedale, it may flood the main road "nearly a yard deep". The Caldew is a fast-flowing river—possibly the fastest in Northern Lakeland. A footbridge near the The Round House, the first reliable crossing point of the river, was in such a decrepit state that some users moved across the rotten decking on hands and knees. The repair work was carried out by the owners of The Round House, who own the road leading to the bridge. Walkers are welcome to use it.

The Round House, closest residence to Skiddaw House, is twelve-sided and was made in 1915 of stone taken from the ruined Wellbank Farm. The Caldew is a musical river. On hot summer days, when people sit in the water to cool off, the clinking of stone against stone on the bed of the river is similar to that of the slate musical instrument in Fitz Park Museum at Keswick. The pieces of slate for the musical instrument came from the same area.

THE DASH FALLS

Mr Collingwood, I presume...

MY FAVOURITE museum has kept its Victorian flavour for a century. Named after Ruskin, and based in Coniston Institute, it was until recent times entered through a turnstile which had affinities with a mouse-trap. The visitor opened a door to enter a tiny room illuminated by cold daylight, entering by north-lights, as in textile mills. Such light does not fade the exhibits—the attractive clutterment of objects which hint at what Coniston folk have been doing with themselves over the centuries.

An ambitious extension plan devised by the trustees has been approved by the Lake District Planning Board. The size of the tiny museum will be trebled, affording more space for displaying the Ruskin collection and for mounting exhibitions about the village and its history. I hope that Ruskin's Museum will not lose its Victorian cosiness. At times, passing along its well-filled cases and glass-fronted cupboards, I have felt to have been transported to the old-days, when the great hills were alive with the sound of mining, when the toot of steam whistles came from the railway and the *Gondola*, carrying visitors around Coniston Water. Happily, of the Old Coniston, *Gondola* and Ruskin's Museum remain. A few enthusiasts have kept the enterprise alive. I hope there will be no headlong dash into the age when museums have become somewhat stark and chilling: statements made by clever young graphic artists and ambitious professional custodians. Presumably the objects will be kept at an even temperature. For years, the atmosphere in the Ruskin museum has been neither too hot nor too dry. Some vintage pipes extended round the room. A curator explained: "When there is heat in the main Institute in the winter, a little bit of it trickles through to the Museum. But the effect is negligible."

It was at the Ruskin Musum, Coniston, that I came face to face with a man who became one of my heroes. I refer to William Gershom Collingwood, writer, artist and one-time secretary to John Ruskin. Handsome, moustached, he was modelled in plaster by his daughter Barbara. This striking piece of sculpture shows him holding a pencil—a real pencil, lightly covered with plaster. A portrait of a younger Collingwood, high on a wall in the Museum, confirms that he was a handsome, positive man.

He was also multi-talented, filling his life with acts of creation, one of which was this little Museum. Collingwood was among those who, in 1895, purpose-built this repository of Times Past as an adjunct to the new Institute. A century later, as I stood before his sculpture in silent homage to a great man, the Trustees were recording an annual attendance of between 7,000 and 8,000 visitors.

Officially, Collingwood was Ruskin's secretary and among his writings is the two-volume biography of the eminent Victorian philosopher and art critic—a study which is sympathetic but sound. Collingwood designed Ruskin's memorial cross in the churchyard and was himself buried in that yard when his notable life ended. The Coniston of W G Collingwood took in the last twenty years or so of Victoria's reign, when "Cunniston", as the native calls it, was developing as a tourist centre after a long spell of as a frontier boom town, its activity and wealth based on mining for copper. A visitor might see old miners and quarrymen, who were always ready to yarn about the old days. The railway brought a thousand people at a time on outings.

Due in no small measure to Collingwood's influence, Coniston became, early in the twentieth century, the artistic centre of the Lake District. Annual exhibitions held in the Institute were supported by artists from a wide area. It was art which first attracted me to W G Collingwood and, in due course, as I planned a holiday bird-watching in Iceland, Bill

Rollinson drew my attention to a rather special link between the Lakes and that astonishing island which abuts the Arctic.

Collingwood was a student of the Icelandic tongue—an interest which may have developed through his friendship with an authority, the Rev Thomas Ellwood, Rector of Torver. When Collingwood was thirty-three years old, in 1897, he had a hectic tour of Iceland on ponyback and recorded, in about 300 sketches and paintings, the life of Icelanders on the saga-steads. This forms a unique record of the period. Collingwood distributed some pictures among those who provided him with hospitality. Most have been assembled as a national collection, on view in Reykjavik.

For the 1897 visit, Collingwood was in the company of an Icelandic scholar, Dr Jon Stefansson. They travelled mainly in the south and west. The journey was recorded in their book, *A Pilgrimage to the Saga-steads of Iceland,* published in 1899. I saw a copy of the work at the home of friends living near Reykjavik. The imprint indicated that the work had been published by W Holmes, Lightburne Road, Ulverston.

Stimulated by the Collingwood sculpture in the Ruskin Museum, by his academic reputation (he became Editor of the *Transactions* of the Cumberland and Westmorland Antiquarian Society) and by his colourful and lively paintings of Lakeland, I inquired into the life and times of William Gershom Collingwood. His father, William, was a well-known landscape painter who had undertaken sketching tours of the Lakes. W G was born in Liverpool in 1864. He became acquainted with John Ruskin at Oxford. Collingwood wife, Edith Isaac, the daughter of an Essex corn merchant, charmed all who met her. They and the children were energetic and talented. The son, Robin George, became a celebrated philospher and historian of Roman Britain.

W G was a most stylish writer, as evidenced by this novel, *Thurston of the Mere,* which deals with Norse times in the Coniston area and, more particularly, by *The Lake Counties* (first published in 1902 and revised by him in 1932). This book was one of a series illustrated by A Reginald Smith. Hugh Walpole wrote in *The Times:* "A friend of mine has described it as 'the finest guide-book in English'; but it is, of course, far more than a guide-book, for it contains the grandest prose-writing about the Lake District in existence...." The opening sentence gives a hint of that style: "Through a gap, for a moment, as the train runs north from Lancaster, there is a peep of the sand, and—far away—the first of the mountains!"

Collingwood had a light touch, was never stilted and just as interested in people as in places. Reading about Coniston, we are introduced to John Beever of the Thwaite, author of *Practical Fly-Fishing*. Across the lake is Tent Lodge, "where Tennyson spent his honeymoon". Behind it is Tent Cottage, the home of Elizabeth Smith (b. 1776, d. 1806), a remarkable and precocious girl, who taught herself a dozen languages while she was still in her 'teens. And at Monk Coniston lived Mr James Garth Marshall, MP for Leeds, "one of the first scientific students of the metamorphic rocks of these mountains" who had made "some valuable contributions to geology." Professor Adam Sedgwick, one of the founders of geology, did much of his pioneering researches into the earth's crest within sight of Coniston Old Man.

Coniston was a tourist's village in Collingwood's time, but the summer coaches passed Monk Coniston Tarns (now widely known as Tarn Hows), "where the mountains peep over the moorland at a charming sheet of water artificially enlarged by a dam...the prettiest bit can only be got at on foot, down the path from the dam, which leads to Tom Gill or, as it is often called nowadays, Glen Mary: I believe somebody has even gone so far as to christen it St Mary's Glen."

Collingwood makes mention of John Ruskin, of course. For nearly twenty years, Ruskin worked at Brantwood "and for ten years more waited there as a worn-out invalid, until death released him (20th January, 1900)." He is remembered by "the tall greenstone cross" which marks his grave.

Autumn

Strangers usually retire with the butterflies; they are seldom seen in October.

William Green of Ambleside (1760-1823).

In November, the silence and solitude of the upper fells seem to infect the whole Lake Country.

Canon H D Rawnsley (1906).

FELL FOOT, LITTLE LANGDALE

THIS FARMHOUSE near the foot of Wrynose Pass has a porch resting on stilts, which makes it distinctive among the old dwellings of Lakeland. In the period from 1640 to 1750, many homes and outbuildings, constructed of timber with wattle-and-daub, were replaced by sturdy, unpretentious buildings fashioned from the locally quarried stone and slate. This new Stone Age followed the liberalisation of trade after the Dissolution of the Monasteries, bringing into being a proud and independent yeoman class of farmer. In due course, there was spare cash for building projects. Creating stone houses was also stimulated by a feeling of security following the end of the Border conflict.

Hot Pot and Herdwicks

RAIN SWEPT up the Troutbeck Valley, near Windermere, with such weight and frequency I could not be certain just where earth met sky. The water seething down the fellsides had the whiteness of spilt milk. Khaki-tinted torrents poured from the lanes. Water accumulating in the dale itself had the dull grey appearance of old pewter. I could not decide, as I approached the *Queen's Head Hotel* for a Shepherds' Meet who was the most disconsolate—the farmers or the sheep.

In 1963, the custom of meeting at a specific place to deal with stray sheep taken up during the autumn "gather" was in decline. It was no longer needed except as an opportunity for farmers to meet, mingle and mull over local affairs over a glass of ale or a plate of tatie-pot. Most of the sheep were herdwicks, of t'auld breed. Small, big-boned, with faces white as hoar frost and bodies swathed in coarse wool, which used to be woven as the celebrated "hodden grey", they had eyes which looked half as old as time.

They might look alike but a Lakeland shepherd could see subtle differences in appearance and gait. He also had recourse to the lug and smit marks. The lug is an ear. Since Norse times it has been customary to clip pieces from an ear to distinguish one flock from another. When, at a Lakeland show, the gate-keeper placed a rubber stamp against the back of my left hand to indicate I had paid, he added that I should consider myself lucky he had not taken a piece out of my left ear! Burning letters on the horn of a tup is another means of identification. And there's the dye used to mark a fleece—again, each mark distinctive and associated with a specific farm. In the old days, tar was used but then the woolmen of

Bradford complained it would not scour out of the wool at the mills.

Propped on the shelf of a Lakeland farm, beside the Bible, is the *Shepherd's Guide*, with its stylised sheep, each showing the farm's identification marks. Fell-going sheep usually remain on their native heafs, even if walls or wire fences are absent. Some straying occurs at the edges. At the "gather", a farmer usually finds himself with one or two of his neighbour's sheep. The neighbour might live in the next dale—hence the custom of all the farmers meeting at some mutually handy spot, preferably a pub. In a world of mobile or static telephones, fax machines and short-wave radio, a Shepherds' Meet is no longer necessary.

In t'auld days, farmers or their men walked the sheep long distances to and from the Meets. Custom decreed that a man who did not turn up to claim a sheep which belonged to him was fined a small sum. Old men tell of a Meet held on High Street, over 2,000 ft above sea level. The event was moved to the *Traveller's Rest* on the summit of Kirkstone Pass, thence—with the passage of years—to the *Queen's Head,* where (over thirty years ago) I joined in the proceedings.

A dripping man entered the bar, emerged from a cocoon of oilskins and sought a place at the fire, where flames flickered against king-sized logs. Another farmer was unwilling to believe that Anthony Chapman had "lowsed" his Coniston foxhounds on to the fells on such a morning. The hounds had been last heard of as they roused a fox on Robin Crag. A devoted hunt supporter commented: "I'd hev thowt Anthony'd hev just gon yam...It's going to be terrible. Hardly fit for sheep." Anthony appeared, soaked but cheerful. He was soon awa' again, following the hounds, with John Bulman in attendance. John had 13 couple hounds of the Windermere Harriers in a van but had decided not to release them in case any sheep which were paniced dashed into storm-swollen becks.

In the previous year, the valley had been crusted with snow

and ice. The *Queen's Head* was cut off by drifts for three chilling days. It had also been a bleak wintry day when the Troutbeck Mayor's Hunt had taken place in February. Now, with teeming, tippling precipitation, and a prospect of flooded roads, business was being carried out urgently, with much commuting between the car park and fireside. Men soon had the inner warmth of ale and good spirits. Helpers at the hotel, and the wives of farmers, attended to the making of a savoury Tatie-Pot, using a cauldron into which they had lowered 40 lb of mutton, a hundredweight of potatoes, three stones each of carrots and onions, and about twenty black puddings.

The bar had an old-world appearance, having been fashioned from an Elizabethan four-poster bed which stood in Appleby Castle. Oak beams, newly exposed after Victorian wallpaper was stripped from them, luxuriated in the fire's heat. Above the main fireplace was a wrought-iron canopy made by George Reed, the Windermere blacksmith, who had welded to it a collection of real horseshoes. To the left of the fireplace, "mine-host" had laid bare a beehive-shaped oven in which bread was once baked. The old spice oven had been restored. Someone told the old story of the man who, asked what he thought of recent alterations, replied: "They're all reet—but I misses t'spittoon." One of his friends laughed and remarked: "Tha allus did!"

Into the Queen's Head, on the day of the Shepherds' Meet, crowded over 100 people who talked and drank and sang until their throats were dry, when they began another round of drinking. I heard "a real bit o' Westmorland twang." A shepherd invited me to take a close look at the gathering. "In another fifty year—'appen less—you'll see nowt like this." A farmer from Crook had risen from his bed at six o' clock, and after mucking-out and foddering his stock had splashed his way to Troutbeck on a motor bike. The grizzle-grey man I next met was Isaac Greenhow, for many years a shepherd in the old tradition. His grandfather, William, was shepherd for

for the ancient Holmes family, "an' that's going back a bit."

Jim Beaty, of Long Green Head, turned up with a single stray sheep—a Rough Fell, which had wandered from the slaty Howgills. Jim, a Mardalian, had tales to tell of the valley before The Flood. They interested me because, in advance of the Meet, I had been re-reading Canon Rawnsley's account of the Mardale Meet as it was early in the century. On the third Saturday in November, the valley had "a gay good getherin' o' fwoke fra far and near". All the beds at the *Dun Bull* had been booked by visitors from Manchester, so Rawnsley had found himself overnight accommodation at a nearby farm. He would be able to dine and enjoy a cosy fire at the *Dun Bull*. On the eve of the Meet, tea consisted of haverbread oatcake, cheese, teacakes, jam and apple pasty. Mine-host had also prepared a rib-stretching Tatie Pot.

Next morning, the Mardalians and their guests awoke to find the dale had been whitened by a heavy "rag" frost. Breakfast consisted of poddish, ham and sausage. The sheep, driven into the garth at the rear of the hotel, were quickly identified. What struck Rawnsley was the quickness of eye which, in a sea of faces, could detect instantly a particular mark or cropped ear. When the sheep were sorted, to everyone's satisfaction, the collies seemed as proud and pleased as their masters. Joe Bowman lowsed (released) the hounds at Grove Brae Farm and they went across Branstreet towards the head of the dale. Three of them were soon back—with the fox in front of them! The hunt lasted three hours. Rawnsley wrote: "The fox deserved better treatment, for he had brought the hunters back to their dinner table almost to a moment. Such a dinner! Beef boiled and roast, plum-pudding and mince pies."

A knot of younger shepherds competed against each other in a clay-pigeon shoot, the "clays" being released by catapult. "Bang went the guns and the clay pigeons generally lived to fly again." But already (ninety years ago!) the simplicity of the time-out-of-mind Shepherds' Meet in the wilderness had been lost, never to return, in the face of "Manchester jovialities" and "Hurlingham hospitalities". Rawnsley's pessimistic view about the future of the Meets was not to be borne out by events; they would linger on in the old spirit until quite recent times.

At Troutbeck, in 1963, Lakeland's version of the Hot Pot, served in the Mayor's Parlour, brought a stampede of flockmasters to where a meal of grand proportions was ready. A glance indicated that it might be a day or two before our ribs would settle back into place. There was a long table, adorned with the usual cutlery and also with huge jars of pickles, piccalilly and beetroot. The Tatie-Pot was as thick as the poddish (porridge) mentioned in an old account—poddish so thick that a mouse might walk dryshod across it. Following the poddish were pie and custard, followed in turn by good strong tea.

The business of the strays was satisfactorily sorted out. The fox put up on Robin Crag was lost. The hounds had been counted out and counted in, without discrepancy. Sodden hunters returned cheerfully to the hotel. For some who attended the Shepherds'' Meet it was not the end but the beginning. The singing and the drinking now began...

Those Terrible Knitters

A clever lass in Dent
Knaws how to sing and knit,
Knaws how to carry the kit (milk pail)
While she drives her kine to pasture.

AT DENT, which became part of the new county of Cumbria in 1974, Betty Hartley and Elizabeth Middleton keep alive the spirit of the old hand-knitters. Clad in traditional clothes, and wielding knitting-sticks and needles, they show something of the agility of that clever lass in Dent, knitting like automata—for such was the Dent way, with not a minute to waste—and meanwhile chatting about the old domestic craft to anyone who will listen. Betty told me: "We don't dress up like those who appear on the stage; we just want people today to know what hand-knitting was all about..."

It was a skill associated with sheep-rearing areas—an ancient skill which, in the sixteenth century, was practised in Cumbria as well as Yorkshire. The change from distaff to spinning wheel allowed a single spinner to provide enough yarn to keep four or five knitters busy. Lakeland's so-called "spinning galleries", seen at such places as Tilberthwaite and Hartsop, may have been used by spinsters or were nothing more than a convenient way of giving access to the upper floors of an outbuilding or for hanging cloth after it had been finished.

With Kendal as a major wool centre, the Westmorland dales had a strong knitting tradition, though Dent's reputation was best-known. So it was that Lakeland lasses might be sent to Dent for training. Among them, at a time lang gone, were Betty and Sally Yewdale, from Langdon (Langdale).

When Betty was an old lady she told her story to Sara Hutchinson, the sister of Mrs William Wordsworth. Sarah wrote it down, as near to how Betty had spoke it.

We recall the Dent knitters because Southey, in his novel called *The Doctor,* used the memorable expression "terrible knitters 'e Dent". In this context, the word terrible means great, not shoddy. The Dent folk did not knit for fun. When the weekly delivery of wool was made by cart from Kendal—the service began at the end of the 18th century and lasted for about 90 years—there was an urge to knit stockings, jerseys, mittens and gloves to supplement a miserable income on a little upland farm. As James Walton, who studied Dales crafts, wrote: "Hand-knitting at Dent was a task cold and hard like the granite masses which surround the village and impart their stubborn, dour character to the natives themselves."

The coarsely-spun wool brought by the weekly cart was known as "bump". A bump-knitter rocked backwards and forwards (also crooning a song) as her nimble fingers handled the four curved metal needles. One needle was slipped into a hole at the end of a dagger-like knitting stick (known in other areas as a sheath) which was held firm by a leather belt. William Howitt (1844) wrote of Dent knitters who sat "rocking to and fro like so many weird wizards. They burn no candle but knit by the light of the peat fire. And this rocking motion is connected with a mode of knitting peculiar to the place, called swaying..."

At Dent, reported Sally Yewdale, a Maister an' Mistress had "larnt us our lessons, yan a piece—an then we o' knit as hard as we cud drive, strivin, which cud knit t'hardest, yan against anudder...We hed our Darrocks (day's work) set afore we come fra' heam in t'mornin'; an' if we deedn't git them dunn we warrant to gang to our dinners..." A song, featuring the names of local people, stimulated them to knit at the required speed. Betty Yewdale observed: "Sally an me wad niver ca' Dent fwoak, seea we ca'ed Langdon fwoak." As follows:

Sally an' I, Sally an' I,
For a good pudding pie,
Taa hoaf wheat, an' tudder hoaf rye,
Sally an' I, for a good pudding pie.

This was sung with an alteration of names at every needle; "an' when we coom at end cried 'off' an' began again, an' sea we strave on, o' t'day through. Neet an' Day ther was nought but this knitting." One snowy night, they ran away, spending the night at an inn at Sedbergh, followed by shelter in the home of a poor woman at Kendal. Here they slept in her room and watched and listened wide-eyed as she had fits! It was during the following night that they reached Langdale, footsore and hungry.

There were lots of children like them—frail, over-exploited but determined. It just so happened that Betty and Sally's story became known to the Wordsworths, and that it was also heard by Southey, the Poet Laureate, who recorded it. Two lile lasses from Gurt Langdon (Great Langdale) are among the immortals!

THE LANGDALE PIKES

The Photographers

CAMERAS were a novelty in Lakeland when Henry Herbert arrived in Bowness to work for Brunskills who, in the 1880s, were well established as photographers. Henry had soon started up his own business, with a staff of ten, and the family name began to appear on the first of many thousands of photographs which, collectively, form an almost complete pictorial record of Bowness during heady years of development.

The family interest in photography had begun with Henry's father, Robert, who was a professional working from a studio in Silver Street. Robert needed brawn as well as skill. The cumbersome plate cameras were at times taken out-of-doors, together with a mobile dark room, which was needed for sensitising the photographic plates and subsequently developing them before they dried out. (Thus the Herbert family invested in a small cart to transport the equipment). The dark-room consisted of a small tent on a tripod. The base of the tent could be tied around the photographer's waist to ensure his work-area was light-proof. The small amount of light admitted was filtered through a small red window and did not affect the plates.

In the studio, before electric light was available, exposures of several seconds' duration were common and in the absence of an enlarger the photographer used large plates—twelve by ten or even fifteen by twelve inches. Frank Herbert, who had begun photography in 1904, and was in partnership with his brother Louis, told me that when he was a small boy, in the winter of 1894-5, Herberts obtained spectacular photographs. Windermere was frozen from end to end for six weeks and at one time about 100,000 people ventured on to the ice. Visitors who came to the district later found it impossible to get rooms even in Kendal because of the demand for accommodation. Skating conditions were perfect because the lake had not frozen over until the snow had ceased. Ice yachts and even a coach and four were able to move on ice estimated to have a depth of nine inches.

The coming of electricity transformed the lives of professional photographers. Exposures were shorter. The clamps which had been attached to the heads of fidgetty customers were no longer needed. The printing process was now free of weather conditions. In the old days, when printing photographs, the sensitive paper had to be placed in frames behind the plates and given a protracted exposure to sunlight. Victorians craved for light. In Frank's young days, the street lighting at Bowness was of the carbon type, which emitted a faint glow which was officially assessed as being of eight candle-power. Frank said he would have preferred the eight candles! Bowness, more progressive than most towns, was the second place in England to have its street lights electrified.

Among the pioneer photographers in Lakeland was George Perry Abraham, born in London in 1846 and trained by Elliott and Fry. He travelled to Keswick to help Alfred Pettit for a season, liked what he saw and, with the help of Mark Shearman, set up as a photographer in a little wooden shop at the corner of Lake Road. He married a local girl, Mary Dixon, and they had two sons, George and Ashley, who followed on in the family business. They were to be specially associated with the new sport of rock-climbing, for which the usual garb worn consisted of Norfolk jackets and knickerbockers. Abraham photographs portrayed climbers performing courageous feats on the crags.

Edward Sankey, who began taking photographs in 1903, had his works in Barrow-in-Furness and annually printed about half a million photographs for the tourist trade. W C Lawrie went in for bird photography at a time when cumbersome equipment had to be moved about the fells. The Misses Slingsby were in business at Grange-over-Sands prior to the First World War. And just afterwards, Mary C Fair of Holmrook, Eskdale, was busy with her camera, portraying ordinary folk at work.

Joseph Hardman, one of the most outstanding of the Lakeland photographers, carried the Victorian and Edwardian tradition of plate cameras into modern times. He came into my life in 1951, when I began to edit the magazine *Cumbria*. Once or twice a month, he sent me a batch of Lakeland photographs. People still discuss or even argue about photography. Is it art? The Lakeland pictures taken with an old plate camera by Joseph Hardman, of Kendal, were almost without fail artistic. His first love was for landscape work, though making a living as a press photographer meant people, from bearded shepherds to glamorous nurses from the Westmorland County Hospital who were provided with a day out and a free meal for allowing him to photograph them in Lakeland settings.

Hardman had an acute awareness of directional light, which distinguishes a photograph from what would otherwise be a picture for the record. The big man from Kendal took around with him his own personal shaft of sunlight, or so it seemed. Many a Hardman picture taken on a lack-lustre day benefited from the spotlight effect of a ray of light picking out the principal feature. Once, the Hardman ray settled on the bearded form of Isaac Cookson, shepherd, rimming his head with silver. Another picture had the word "sunbeams" in the title. I marvelled at the delicate effect, achieved in what to me had been the far-from-scintillating medium of monochrome photography.

Hardman photographs are never ordinary, dull or flat. The largest collection is at Abbot Hall, Kendal. With most of his studies, you might tell the time of day and the season of the year. He was, as indicated, a master of against-the-light photography. He put a halo round a fell and a shimmer on the lakes. When I knew him, he had well over 50,000 glass plates and was adding to the stock at the rate of a score or two a week, fifty-one weeks in the year. During the other week, Joseph and Edith, his wife, were on holiday, invariably in Blackpool. Or sunning themselves in the garden at Berner's Close, Grange-over-Sands.

Joseph Hardman was, when I knew him, well into middle-aged, heavily-built but with a face that had the ruddy look of the typical countryman. It radiated cordiality—as, indeed, it must if he was to persuade strangers as well as friends to stand while he captured them on sensitised plates. His photography was also a venture into social history, full of action which sprang from normal events and was not contrived. Even a line-up of three well-known Lakeland sheep farmers looked far from ordinary. At Eskdale show, when rain and mist spoilt the chances of many photographers, Hardman portrayed W Wilson (Herdwick Billy), of Bassenthwaite, W M Wilson, of Glencoin, Ullswater, and J Richardson, of Buttermere, leaning against a sheep-pen, with the white faces of one or two Herdwicks in between. The men were relaxed and the detail of their clothes—trilbies and macks—rendered in satisfying detail. (How was it possible for three standard trilbies to become so individualistic with the passing years?).

Hardman was born at Radcliffe, near Manchester, and at the age of eleven became a half-timer at a factory producing shuttles for the cotton mills. Half the day was spent at school and half at work. He was paid 1s.10d (if he worked afternoons) or 3s.4d (for the mornings). He began working full-time at the age of fourteen but in 1911 he left Lancashire for Kendal, where he became a member of the local Photographic Society. Soon he was devoting all his waking time to photography.

He made an early decision, to please himself what he took rather than to do commercial work, where the customer is the boss. He told me: "When you are taking portraits, the model can talk back. When you're taking a landscape, you can please yourself." He had no interest in driving a car, which is why he hired a taxi or was taken to the Lakes in the car of a friend. "I think I can do better when I'm sitting in the back of the car...I don't miss much then!" He might travel 200 miles a week by taxi, covering all the main Lakeland events and being first to provide the newspapers with pictures of the first clusters of snowdrops or daffodils.

When I met him in 1953 he was preparing to photograph an April event—the movement of a large flock of sheep from their wintering grounds on the Cartmel Fells to their home farms at the head of Wensleydale, over forty miles away. The journey took two days. The sheep passed Kendal Town Hall at twelve noon on the appointed day and reached Sedbergh, the first halt, about five. Each April, therefore, I might expect to receive a Kendal photograph with a difference, the main street (then mercifully less congested with traffic) being packed, kerbstone to kerbstone, with a grey mass of animals. His career was not without incident. He accidentally dropped a valuable camera into the river at Skelwith Falls. He and his wife were once pursued by a bull and managed to scramble over a wall, though Edith lost the contents of her handbag and they had to wait for an hour or so before the bull wearied and walked off.

Joseph Hardman cheerfully admitted he was overweight, tipping the scales at sixteen stones towards the end of his life. At one time, he was three stones heavier than that. He was quite agile but kept walking to a minimum, agreeing with a friend who said he was fond of the fells but preferred to see them framed by his bay window. Edith, to whom he was married for over fifty years, was his helpmate, positioning the heavy tripod to his instructions and generally fussing around until he was ready to release the shutter mechanism. On a good day, he might expose five dozen plates. He then did all his own darkroom work, staying in the dark "until I'm tired". He died in 1972. When I last saw him before his steady decline he spoke movingly about his Lakeland residence. "I wouldn't dream of living and working anywhere else. Lakeland is my very heart and soul."

Walter Poucher, whose work captured the beauty and mood of the mountains, miniaturised the Lakeland photographic routine. This remarkable man, who was born in mountainless Lincolnshire and lived to celebrate his 91st brithday, carried a Leica, of 35 mm format, at a time when such a small camera was not considered good enough for portraying landscape. The reproduction of colour photography is now commonplace and relatively cheap. I look back at the excitement created in Lakeland whenever *Cumbria* used a Poucher picture, printed from a set of copper blocks, across two pages of the magazine. I drooled over it, especially as Walter Poucher never charged us for the use of his work!

His forty year obsession with mountain photography was not his principal work. He qualified as a chemist in 1912 and was for thirty enjoyable years the chief perfumer of Yardley. His first published book, a three-volume work about the synthesis of flower perfumes, appeared in 1923. Being a chemist, when he became interested in photographing mountains— prompted by a paucity in Lakeland of moody mountain pictures—Walter Poucher approached the subject methodically.

He returned to Lakeland with cameras, various makes of good film and every available filter. "I made the exposures throughout the whole, range, from one second to 1,000th of a second." Then he studied the negatives, discovered that the secret of good mountain photography was in the filter, if the exposure was correct, and deduced that the filter to use was a pale orange. Writing about his discovery, he ensured that the country's available stock of orange filters was soon exhausted! A notable exhibition of eighty considerable enlargements of Poucher's work, held in London in 1946, is significant in photographic history. As the photographer himself remarked: "You could say that the show was the birthplace of landscape for the miniature camera."

Walter Poucher recommended a short exposure, asserting that one of the major causes of unclear photographs is camera-shake. He worked at 1/250th of a second for black-and-white and colour and never altered it. He tried to work at about f5.6, the optimum aperture for sharpness. For Poucher, who travelled widely in Europe and America, Lakeland remained a favourite district and some of his later life was spent at Keswick. He had some frustrating moments with the weather and on one visit, when he wished to photograph mountains in rain and cloud, the weather was perverse, the sky remaining clear for nineteen days. His favourite view in Lakeland was Wastwater "because of the peaks which surround its head."

Derry Brabbs's introduction to the Lake District was "courtesy of A W" (Alfred Wainwright). He illustrated several of the books which, based on the early pictorial guides of the master fell-walker, are notable not only for the outstanding photography but the application of modern cameras, lenses, film and the printing technique in a way which had not been possible a few years earlier. Derry got on well with the inscrutible Wainwright and recalled: "Once he knew that I could do what I was supposed to do—and I was doing what he wanted—then the relationship bonded."

A W (as he was known to his close friends) was in the habit of doing his own page-layouts, typing out the manuscripts and leaving spaces for photographs. "It has made life very easy". The difficult bit was securing photographs of sufficiently high quality in a region where the mountains do not always have sunlight upon them...which means that they give out their true colours and textures and all the cracks and crevices are well defined."

Derry's photography is done on 35 mm film. He is sparing in the use of colour filters but does like to fit a graduated grey filter to his camera to bring the sky into parity with the foreground. "Skies, particularly in the Lakes, are to me an integral part of the pictures." He spends most of his time in his own company, acknowledging that mountain photography is a solitary occupation. "No one can help me do it. No one can help me edit photographs because only I know what I am looking for. Really and truly, I'm a solitary sort of person."

BLENCATHRA

Red Deer Roaring

OCTOBER is the month of the "roaring", to use a somewhat romantic Scottish term for a stag announcing his presence during the rut, the time of mating. It is one time of the year when the largest of our terrestrial mammals uses its voice. A visitor to Claife Heights, above Windermere, who heard the "roaring", later reported: "There's a cow bawling it's 'eeard off." To deer-watchers it is a wild, romantic sound. The stag raises its head until its multi-tined antlers are almost digging into its back. Its mouth is shaped like a letter O.

The autumnal roaring has roused the Lakeland echoes for some 6,000 years, since—in the wake of receding ice—the first of the red deer moved into the area. Peter Delap says that to the Mesolithic hunter a red stag was the gastronomic jackpot, representing 300 pounds of prime meat. The Neolithic farmer who succeeded him doubtless thought of deer as one of the marauders which threatened his crops. In medieval times, the ownership of a deer park represented to my lord a store of fresh food—a protein bank, in effect. He could taste venison when lesser mortals had only tough, salted meal at their disposal. The dreams of old-time man were coloured by the thought of sinking his teeth into flesh from so large and succulent a beast as a deer.

Red deer ranged far and wide. In Norman times, forests (land set apart for hunting by the king and his nobles) included Inglewood (west of the Eden, from Penrith to Carlisle), Ennerdale or Coupland (also taking in Wasdale), Walton (on the northern march) and Martindale (in Westmorland). The Abbot and monks of Furness rejoiced when Alice de Romille, taking out a divine insurance for the souls of her family past, present and future, granted them all Borchedale (Borrowdale), with hart and hind, boar and sow, goshawk and sparrow-hawk, and venison and all beasts of game to be found there. The same monks obtained hunting rights on Furness Fells.

The last of the "wild Red Deer" of Inglewood were hunted to their deaths by the Hasells of Dalemain, supported by hounds. They claimed the last stag here and on Whinfell. The Dalemain hounds continued to find stags in remote Martindale, which is still owned by the family, being the only deer-stalking forest in England. It is recorded that towards the end of last century a Scottish stag and a few young hinds were introduced in the hope of improving the "heads", and that feeding troughs had been set out for the deer in severe weather.

Ennerdale Forest, consisting mainly of wild hill country, held some mighty stags. William de Meschin, founder of St Bees, assigned to the monks a tithe of venison. In 1512, the number of red deer in "Wasdale" was computed at 230. A century later, in the "fells and mountains" called Wasdale was "ground full of red deer". In another century and a half, Wasdale and Martindale were the only remaining Lakeland deer forests and in about 1675 Sandford was writing with enthusiasm of the deer of Ennerdale, on the wilder western fells. Here were "as great Hartts and Staggs as in any part of England."

Strange tales of deer were told. Sheep which occasionally wandered on to Pillar in search of fresh herbage were "forked" over the side by the deer and fell about 200 ft to their deaths. The shepherds retaliated by building a wall to keep out both deer and sheep. In Side Wood, on the southern shore of Ennerdale, old scythes and pitchforks were placed in gaps in the fences to keep the deer out of the crops.

The "plastic" quality of the red deer—an ability to adjust size to widely differing locations—means that Lakeland has several types. The Martindale stock occupies the bare ridges and reedy dalehead and extends east and south into what a friend calls Lakeland's Empty Quarter. At the head of Martindale is the hillside bungalow made for Lord Lonsdale when he had the local stalking. Outside, on a post, is the all-important weather vane, for hunters must "watch the wind". The blocky hill nearby is the Nab, where Martindale deer had a quiet retreat until unofficial intrusion by walkers caused them to seek sanctuary in an adjacent valley head.

In Wet Sleddale lies "a buck park", which was studied and described by Peter Delap. He was excited when reading of research elsewhere by Oliver Rackham that such satellite holding-pens were a regular adjunct of Royal Forests. I have visited the spot with the Deer Society. Two large enclosures, flanked by walls which in places are still of considerable height, lie in an area where deer driven from the fells would converge and, following the walls, would enter an enclosure by an ingenious baffle.

Living in Grizedale and South Lakeland are big woodland deer, which have plenty of cover and food through the year. These deer are able to fill out their frames. The stags are sustained by rich feeding in the post-rut period and during the lusty growth of new antlers when they have parted with the old horns in spring. Somewhere in size between the Martindale and woodland deer are the red deer of the Thirlmere area—animals which divide their time between woodland, crag and open fell. In winter, they wait until dusk and then move, as inconspicuously as shadows, to the big fields beside the Keswick road.

To visit Hay Bridge, in the Rusland Valley, when it was the home of Tissie Fooks, was to enter the domain of the big woodlanders. The house was decked with the heads of deer culled by the late Herbert Fooks. The immediate grounds held a captive herd of fallow and, at times, exotics like muntjac. Tissie provided quarters for Josephine, a roe doe, and also a peevish red stag which had been picked up as a calf by a Bowland family having a Scottish holiday. What was at first an attractive little pet deer soon turned into a rampaging adult with horns; hence its banishment to Hay Bridge, where the nature reserve was not originally intended for waifs and strays. Much more exciting was the view from an observation tower of wild stock in field or scrubland.

Once, I combined deer-watching at Hay Bridge with Grizedale Forest, rising at 4 a.m. to motor between the two places. It was a calm morning, after a night of hard frost which had brought down most of the beech foliage of trees flanking the road east of Coniston Water. The wheels of my car created a swishing sound as they disturbed the crisp, autumn-tinted leaves without flattening them. By first light, I was in position to watch a stag with its harem.

A favourite excursion was to climb Raven Crag at Thirlmere. The chilly autumnal air was vibrant with the ill-concealed passion of stags which had the mating fever upon them. These animals had wallowed in an area where they had whipped up the peaty ground into a porridge-like mixture. Wet mornings showed up the grey lichen which plated many of the young conifers. I remember finding an old cast horn beside the gaudy form—red with white spots—of fly agaric. At Thirlmere, during the rut, throaty sounds were heard reverberating against the crumbling faces of Sipling Crag, Raven Crag and Fisher Crag. Far below, Thirlmere had the dull gleam I usually associate with antique pewter. In due course, I would locate deer. Once, when I had two hinds and a calf in view, a 10-point stag seemed to materialise at the edge of the trees. Another time, two stags fought it out at the edge of Fisher Crag. Fighting is a last resort, being a trial of strength rather than an attempt to slay the opponent.

Of the park deer, my favourites were those at Lowther where, as the chestnut trees took on their coats of many colours before the leaf-fall, the big stags roared. The deer were still showing the red of the summer coat. Wallows bore the imprints of limbs, tines, and even a pattern of hair from the body of the beasts that last stirred them up. The big trees were sometimes lacerated by a stag pressing its antlered head against them, leaving on the trunks the vertical scoring which would become conspicuous as they whitened through a fungal infection.

The Lakeland reds are holding their own in spite of poaching, or what a warden friend calls "various nefarious activities". Apart from the areas already mentioned, some movement occurs between Thirlmere in the north and Loughrigg in the south, the animals tending to keep to the west of Grasmere and Rydal. Outliers from Grizedale occur near Coniston and Tarn Hows. A few travelling stags occur in Ennerdale, now a forest in the modern sense of ranks of conifers but, in a Survey of Cumberland drawn up by Sir Daniel Fleming in 1671, "a fforest well stored with deer".

Herries Country

AN AMERICAN reader who did not care for fiction explained: "I'm not that interested in events which did not happen to people who never existed." Hugh Walpole's great Cumberland saga, *Herries Chronicle,* makes imaginery people believable because they and the landscape were fused by the novelist's skill and insight. So while Rogue Herries, Judith Paris and the others are figments of his imagination, his meticulous descriptions of Lakeland scenery are recognisable. Walpole visited the areas he described. He was inclined to "destroy" an important building if there was a chance of it being confused with one standing at the spot he had selected for action.

Herries Country takes in Borrowdale and its surrounding fells. At Grange (named after a monastic outfarm) is the graceful double-bridge spanning the Derwent—a bridge from which, in *Rogue Herries,* Old Mrs Wilson, suspected of being a witch, is tossed to her death through drowning. The site of Brackenburn, his own Lakeland house, overlooking Derwentwater, was used for Adam Paris's abode in *The Fortress*. Rosthwaite was the setting for the somewhat dilapidated Herries home. The *Hazel Bank Hotel* now occupies the site. Watendlath, tucked away among the quiet hills, is still resonant with the doings of the Paris family and boasts of Judith Paris's house.

Stockley Bridge, which arches itself over the beck on the route from Seathwaite to Sty Head, saw an encounter between David Herries and a pedlar with a "sharp bright face" who said he was the Devil. On the shore of the well-named Sprinkling Tarn (in the wettest part of England) David Herries, when eloping with Sarah Denburn, fought with

Denburn and Captain Bann. (The luckless Denburn was hurled into the water). Uldale, back o'Skiddaw, is another Herries haunt. At Wasdale Head, Walpole placed an inn—"a small place... smelling of food, ale, dung, human unwashed bodies"—where, in Herries time, none existed; it was built in the following century.

My introduction to the Herries family and their swashbuckling ways came the hard way—through reading the special, brick-sized Macmillan edition of the *Herries Chronicle*, published in 1939. The four books, consisting of 1,488 pages of text, appeared between the same covers. On receiving his author's copy, Walpole had exultantly written of the bargain it represented—"nearly a million words for 8/6d." Sixty years after their creation, the intending reader of Herries takes the story in easy bites, as individual books.

This natural story-teller, a bachelor with good social connections, bestrode two worlds—the literary and social world of London, where he was feted, and craggy Cumberland, where he came close to squirehood. He was forty years old, and the author of seventeen volumes of "more or less merit", when he discovered Lakeland. In the autumn of 1923, he was driven from London by his friend Douglas Chanter. They spent the first night at Nottingham and by nightfall on the second day had reached Ambleside.

On the third day, at Keswick, a stray remark by a hotelier—that the house Brackenburn, overlooking Derwentwater, was on the market—caused Hugh to delay his further progress to Edinburgh. Having acquired Brackenburn, he had a property which was well-named, with bracken on the fellside and no less than two burns, one of which has not been known to dry up. In the early 1980s, a minor avalanche occurred, about forty tons of material from a freak seam of shale being swept down. A local tradition asserts that if the Grange water supply fails, an unlikely event, local people are permitted to draw water at Brackenburn.

Walpole carried out improvements, built a garage with a

study above it in which he might write and and kept a journal, giving it the grand name of *The Brackenburn Book*. He wrote of his preparations for writing: "I push back the door, get up the stairs to the room that levels the tree-tops, sit down, fuss with my paper and pen, look about me, and then, suddenly, my vision is filled once again with that other world."

Walpole loved solitude but was not basically a hermit. He introduced Brackenburn, his "little paradise on Catbells", to selected friends, including the novelist and playwright J B Priestley—Jolly Jack, who was duly photographed with Walpole in the grounds. The two writers had collaborated in a novel, *Farthing Hall,* ingeniously basing it on an exchange of letters. His share of the income from sales gave Priestley the financial security he needed for writing *The Good Companions,* one of the literary highlights of the 1930s. He dedicated the book to Walpole.

Walpole's friend and biographer, Sir Rupert Hart-Davis, confirmed for me the impression of Walpole as a man who needed each of his worlds and who was bored if he remained in one of them for too long. In all his seventeen years at Brackenburn, Walpole was never there for longer than five weeks at a stretch and very seldom for more than two or three. Needing excitement and the adulation of London, Walpole would slip away to his bachelor flat in London. Then, wearied of London, he would drive to Lakeland, for another spell of walking, directing, contemplation and writing.

Between 1928 and 1932, the Herries, his Cumberland family, took control of him. Walpole set their loves and adventures in the eighteenth century and hoped that they would "do something for this admirable place. I feel a longing desire to pay it back for some of its goodness to me."

The first of the books, *Rogue Herries,* was described by the author as "a fine queer book in the big manner." The succeeding novels were *Judith Paris, The Fortress* and *Vanessa,* followed after a gap by *The Bright Pavilions*. Their setting was the upjutting, craggy, frost-cracked, raven-haunted landscape of the Borrowdale Volcanics and in a burst of self-criticism he wrote of them: "Old-fashioned they certainly are—verbose, over-emphasised, unreal in many places, sometimes very dull, but...they have caught something definite out of both this place and me..." They are not to be rated among the best of English novels, but they contain some memorable characterisations and incidents and, though romantic, they offer a glimpse of the Cumbrian way of life two centuries ago. Regarded as regional fiction, the *Herries Chronicle* might be compared with Scott's *Borderland* and Hardy's *Wessex*.

My last tour of Herries Country was incorporated into an autumnal course on Lakeland writers and artists which I organised at Abbot Hall, the Methodist hotel overlooking Morecambe Bay. Having met Rupert Hart-Davis and read his 500-page biography of the man, I was prepared for briefing those attending the course. I was even familiar with Walpole's normal daily routine—up for breakfast early, and from 8-30 an hour devoted to letter-writing, followed by uninterrupted work on the novel in hand until luncheon. There followed reading or walking, a chat with visitors or a drive in the car.

Our Abbot Hall group ventured to the end of the road at Watendlath, which is tucked away among the lean fells near Borrowdale. With some of our members halt and lame, transport had to be arranged. A luxury coach took us to Keswick. We had arranged a mini-bus shuttle from here to Watendlath. It was an autumn day touched by the lean forefinger of winter. The air was dull, moist and chilling. Derwentwater was grey and gleaming. When Walpole wrote about the lake, "the water whispered with the soft splash of oars." We took to the hills at Ashness, crossed the famous bridge, stopped briefly at the Surprise View (of Derwentwater and Skiddaw). Walpole described the cul de sac as a tract which "could indeed be scarcely named a village, rather it was a narrow strip of meadow and stream lying between the wooded hills."

Eventually we reached Watendlath, in the Judith Paris section of National Trust Country, recalling an old-time rift between two local families, each of whom claimed they were living in Judith's house. (Walpole diplomatically announced that he had no specific building in Watendlath in mind, though it is clear from his description which was intended). The sun does shine at Watendlath, bringing a sparkle to the tarn. When the first flush of grass appears in spring, there is a green carpet to contrast with the dun colours of the fells. They have been gouged into V-shaped gills by heavy rainfall. Autumn wears a coat of many colours and the lower slopes hold the copper of bracken fronds. On the day of our visit, conditions were just dull. The farms and outbuildings seemed to cluster as though for mutual comfort. The novelist used the seclusion of Watendlath to cloak the activities of George Paris, a smuggler (who gets his cum-uppence when he is tossed from a stairway to his sudden death).

No one felt like hanging about at Watendlath, where, not long after he had begun *Judith Paris*, Walpole, his brother Robin and sister Dorothea had a picnic. By permission, we visited Brackenburn, Walpole's house, which is not normally open to the public. Brackenburn, a slate house built for the Richardson family only fourteen years before, has almost an acre of steep and soggy garden behind, rock plants and ornamental shrubs before and a pleasant lawn. In the *Brackenburn Book*, Walpole listed some of the features: "Running stream, garden, lawn, daffodils, squirrels, music-room, garage, four bedrooms, bath—All!" As a celebrity, he attracted visitors who, he wrote in the summer of 1932, "peer into my windows, invade my garage, discuss my books loudly and so on."

The garage and writing-room (now known as Brackenburn Lodge), carry a circular plaque commemorating the Walpole associations. The garage doors are painted blue. The building received a light-hearted mention in the novel *Vanessa,* where one of the characters, after explaining the fictional building was owned by a novelist, wished he had not used blue paint on the doors. The upper room of this sturdy, detached building served Walpole as a library and study, its walls, where they were not adorned by paintings, including work by Cezanne, Picasso and Gaugin, being lagged with 30,000 books.

We were shown what had been the drawing room, with a long, angled mirror above the fireplace, so that anyone sitting facing the fire could, simultaneously, see a reflection of the wide sweep of Derwentwater. It was rather like using a Claude glass, beloved of early tourists, who turned their back on their favourite tracts of landscape and, by peering in the glass, and moving it about, were able to compose pretty pictures. In the kitchen, the tap was left running until water, clear and sparkling as wine brought up from the cellar, might be poured into glasses to assuage our thirsts.

My most recent view of Herries Country was from Maiden Moor, as I walked towards Catbells. In a sweeping glance, I beheld lake, dale, fells, oakwoods, scattered buildings, the highest land having snow in its joints. Early in the eighteenth century, when the Herries story began, "there's not a cart in Borrowdale, brother, nor a road to carry one. It's all horseback round here...You wanted cheap living and you've got it. Naked bottom and bare soil!" Not until 1842 was a good road made through the Jaws into Borrowdale, replacing the old high level packhorse track which brought life and some trade to Watendlath.

Walpole died aged fifty-seven. A Celtic cross marks his grave in St John's churchyard, Keswick. He chose his own last resting place, of which he had written: "The view from the churchyard was superb...In front, the hills, just touched with rose; behind, the little grey street, quite silent, thin spirals of smoke coming from the chimneys..."

Sphinx Rock and Napes Needle

THE ONLY clouds in the sky formed a ragged line over the Pennines, where a light north-easterly, cooled on its progress up the slopes, was meeting the warmer air of the Eden Valley. Colin and I had intended to park the car near Seathwaite Farm but settled instead for a section of verge a third of the way to Seatoller. There was time for a word with Stanley Edmondson, whose family have farmed at Seathwaite for many years. When I first knew Seathwaite, there would have been blank looks if I had asked for him. Four Stanleys, of successive generations, were living at the wettest inhabited spot in England.

We walked to the beck under the steely gaze of Herdwicks. We did not walk alone and had to queue at the bridge over the beck. Then we were on our own for a while, climbing beside tumbling water and on rocks which had some ice in their joints. A party of students from Manchester overtook us. A girl with flaming red hair, round face and toothy smile might have been Fergie (the Media name for the Duchess of York) if we had not recently seen a photograph of her on the Himalayas. We left the well-trodden route to Green Gable by swinging left to climb a boulder slope to Base Brown, pausing to look at the Hanging Rock, which is said to have a cavity beneath it. Wadd pilfered from the Seathwaite plumbago mines was kept until it was safe to take it away from the district. Or so the old folk tell us...

The view of Seathwaite from the rim of Base Brown took in the farm, with its neat pattern of drystone walls and, on a mound behind the farmhouse, traces of much older field boundaries. I wondered if these had been made by the Norsefolk of over a thousand years ago whose "thwaite" this was. On my last visit, I had seen the glint of water. Everywhere was the glint of floodwater. The average rainfall at Seathwaite is about 120 inches a year, with 200 inches or more on the neighbouring fells. One of the Stanley Edmondsons told me: "July and August can be terribly wet up here. One August, water got into the house. It was three feet deep in the living room."

Base Brown fell to us without a murmur. We trudged on to Green Gable, via a wide, eroded track which must be the fell-top equivalent of the M.6. When Gable looked tantalisingly near, we slid into Windy Gap, where patches of snow linger well into the spring and the view included Ennerdale, with its lagging of conifers. Our gaze returned to Gable. More precisely, to the top of this massive red pyramid. To Eliza Lynn Linton, a Victorian visitor, Gable's careworn appearance was impressive—"a whole cascade of immense boulders pouring from that sweeping curve to show what wind and rain have done." This is the fell which, viewed from Wasdale, has classical lines, as though it was designed by an artist rather than being the result of a rough-and-tumble in a geological playground.

Walkers who were studying a map—an excuse for a rest before climbing Great Gable—were startled as we went clatteringly off on the Girdle, exchanging sunshine for shadow and a reasonable path for one which undulated and was marked for much of its length simply by the white bruising where rocks had rubbed together under booted feet. We decided to "pop" up Kirk Fell for a snack meal. It was the last time either of us used the word "pop" for the climb was a struggle. A cheerful couple from Whitehaven told us about Kirk Fell when it was being sped across by fell-runners.

We celebrated reaching the summit, at 2,630 ft, with the last of the thermos tea. Our return to the Gable Girdle, via the grassy (and squelchy) finger of Beckhead, was also a return to the rocky track. Wasdale, with its spider's web wall-pattern, was laid out as though it were a model on a planner's table. Wastwater was winking back at the sun. Most of the time, we kept our eyes on the track. Having crossed a formidable scree slope, Colin announced we were going to leave the main track for the "scenic route". Almost immediately we were scrambling on rocks—a finger-end bruising, boot-jamming business. He went ahead, into a world of sunlit rock turrets, some with overhangs. Colin gave a cheerful whoop on finding Cat Rock (known to W A Poucher as The Sphinx). I struggled up, passing well-equipped climbers on passage to their favourite crags.

Soon I was standing beside an elated Colin, who held a camera to his eye. He was about to "snap" the celebrated piece of natural sculpture in perfect conditions. The late afternoon sunshine which illuminated Wasdale far below had thrown the rock into deep shadow. I thought Cat Rock looked like the head of a Red Indian brave, keeping eternal vigil over Wasdale Head, which lay flatly between the billowing slopes of Lingmell (my last "Wainwright") and the blocky form of Yewbarrow, up the near vertical snout of which I climbed with much grunting and puffing. Ilgill Head, which terminates in the fearsome screes above Wastwater, resembled an inverted pudding basin.

Colin and I recovered our concentration on matters close to hand. A goat-like scramble brought us to near the base of Napes Needle, which was climbed in 1886 by W P Haskett-Smith, an excursion said to mark the start of Lakeland's "golden age" of mountaineering. (In 1936, Haskett-Smith made a jubilee ascent of the famous stack). Colin proved to be more adventurous than me, a mere fell-walker.

Graham Sutton, the novelist who lived Underskiddaw, wrote a celebrated short story about The Man Who Broke the Needle. (His harrowing ascent of England's best-known rock pinnacle to the last precariously perched lump of stone turned out to be a fantasy climb, at the dentist's, and the "climber" came abruptly back to reality when the voice of a dentist was heard apologising because the hypodermic needle had broken).

I saw the Needle festooned with members of the Durham University climbing club and their gear. Anyone who passes between the Needle and its parent cliff is said to have gone through the Needle's eye. Colin elected to do this. Before I left him, he was climbing diminutive holds, at the approaches to the "eye". My next sighting was at t'other side as he descended a rock with few holds—and deftly caught the helmet of a climber which had been inadvertently dropped from above. Collingwood, in his stylish guide, *The Lake Counties* (1902), wrote of Napes Needle: "For a mere fell-walker, there is reward in beholding it near at hand, abrupt upon the slope, with the Isle of Man in the distance above the deep valley."

The fellsides were now banded with shadow. We did our boulder-jumping routine and were overtaken by the Durham climbers, who were now actually running. We located the main track near Sty Head. The tarn held a mirror-reflection of Great End. The flood of walkers heading back for Seathwaite had become a trickle. We arrived at the wettest cluster of buildings in England just in time to celebrate our achievements with a long, cold drink.

Borrowdale Oakwoods

ON MY Coast to Coast Walk I spend a day in the Wilderness and descended, on a golden evening, into the Promised Land of Borrowdale. Having arranged to spend the night at Stonethwaite, I followed the trod through Johnny's Wood, elated by being in the company of venerable oak trees, in one of the woods classified by the Nature Conservancy Council as "clearly among the first echelon of Grade 1 sites." Around me were sessile oaks, the oaks of the North Country, so named because they have unstalked acorns. The leaves themselves are long-stalked, with wedge-shaped bases. On my walk in the Promised land I also saw the well-known lobed leaf of an oak on signs which signified that the tracts of land are owned by The National Trust.

When, in spring, the thin voices of the warblers are heard under a sunlit canopy of leaves, and there is no obvious sign of human activity beyond the eroded path, it is not difficult to imagine our Lakeland dales clothed in an almost continuous wood with oak as the main species—oak descended from those which rooted among the screes as the landscape began to green-up following glaciation, each leaf-fall contributing to the development of a rich humus on which other plants might grow.

The oakwoods of Borrowdale extend to the banks of the Derwent, the name of which means "oak river". The climax forest, haunt of wolf and bear, was attained thousands of years ago. In Neolithic times, around 2000 BC., man was striving towards the creation of a landscape which would suit him, and in the process he used the Great Cumberland Axe (made of volcanic tuff from Pike o' Stickle) in order to clear areas for settlement and farming. For centuries, the local woodland was kept young by periodic clear-felling to provide charcoal for iron-smelting, bark for tanning and the raw material for a dozen woodland crafts. Now, no long intensively worked, many oakwoods have a natural appearance. Trees, being allowed to develop in their various locations, have become as individualistic and characterful as the dalesfolk themselves.

Borrowdale's oak trees dominate the valley. Yellow autumn sunlight slants through a multi-coloured canopy. But the oaks have the support of a glorious "mix" of indigenous trees, including the hazel (which in springtime produces clouds of yellow blossom), ash, alder and birch (especially common around the Bowder Stone). To the Wordsworths, William and Dorothy, this romantic valley was noted especially for its yews, a group of four comprising what William termed a "gloomy grove". His sister Dorothy, having described an ascent to the Top of Scafell, travelled home by horse-drawn cart in the moonlight, passing the famous Borrowdale Yews, an experience she recorded in her *Journal*. William wrote that Borrowdale "surpasses all others in variety" with its "Rocks and Woods...intermingled on the hillsides with profuse wildness..."

After many years during which Borrowdale, in common with much of Lakeland, was coppiced for industrial or craft purposes, the oakwoods were left to themselves, being at the mercy of hungry mammals, including sheep and deer, which prevent natural regeneration. Walk through the oakwoods today—as you might, without much effort, from Grange-in-Borrowdale to Rosthwaite, returning via the Bowder Stone—and you will find gnarled veterans, rooted among rock and upstanding oldies, which had a better start in life. Also in view are fenced-off tracts of young trees, the nucleus of a Borrowdale oakwood of the future.

A few days spent with friends at Grange-in-Borrowdale had re-introduced me to the pleasures of the Oakwoods. In summer, there is a saturation of green. In the early morning, the woods seem to be as damp, green and mysterious as an Amazonian jungle. The oaks of Johnny's Wood have grey-barked trunks which send out a radiating cluster of branches. Their domed crowns may be admired at close quarters from the rim of a crag against which a tree has grown. Like the dalesmen, the oaks cling to the landscape, determined not to be dislodged. In Johnny's Wood, many of the trees have rooted in deep clefts and crannies of the rocks, which hereabouts are green over with mosses and ferns. These include lady fern, growing on tree stumps; polypod and beech fern, to me the most attractive of the family.

The crags ring with the metallic calls of jackdaws. By the river are grey wagtails and dippers, the latter doing their press-ups on the boulders. Rising above the jungle-like spread of oaks, and bristling with pines, is Castle Crag, a cone-shaped hill, re-shaped and littered by slate-quarrymen. Castle Crag is a superb vantage point from which to overlook Borrowdale and Derwentwater. They do say that Borrowdale men built a wall across the bottom end of the dale—to prevent the cuckoo from leaving and taking the good weather with it. Good weather is sunny weather, of course. Bad weather, or rain, nourishes the oakwoods, gives the dale its lush appearance and keeps Derwentwater topped up.

Wasdale Show

WE WENT to Wasdale Head the hard way—across the grain of the landscape, via the high passes of Wrynose and Hardknott. Stretches of tarmac bore the black marks where drivers had been standing on their brakes. I saw score-marks from low cars which had never before encountered such a road, with its stiff gradient, adverse camber, jay-walking sheep and low-flying aircraft. The fells were bronzed by dying bracken fronds. The blowlamp of the sun had dried the rock outcrops. The odd cloud seemed to be looking for a way around the peaks. Fell-walkers, wearing mud-flaps, headed into the landscape.

My companions, Ian and Pat Lewthwaite, have lots of relations in the west. They had been this way many times before. I felt the old elation at mountaineering on four wheels. And I recalled a story told to me by John Wyatt, first of the National Park wardens, who watched a saloon car being reversed off one of the steepest bits and, talking to the pale and nervously-strung-up driver, was asked: "Is this the way to Blackpool?" We stopped for a bar-snack, then returned to the narrow, winding roads of the West. We were on our way to one of Lakeland's great social occasions—Wasdale Show, an autumn event. Soon we were in nodding range of the most famous Lakeland trinity of fells—Gable, Kirk Fell, Scafell, these three, and the greatest of these (to me) is Gable.

Wasdale enfolded as a strip of tarmac, flanked by rocks, bracken and guzzling sheep, with fells to the left and Wastwater to the right. Rising beyond Wastwater, with all the drama of a piece of scenery in a Wagnerian opera, were The Screes, like a series of giant fans, with boulders which looked football-sized from a distance but at close range would be found to be as large as the family car. Soon our attention had switched to the high fells and Pat was asking (without the expectation of a reply) if any of us could think of a finer view on such a bonny morning as this.

Wasdale Head is a thinly-spread community in which each person is a character, someone with an individualistic point of view, which is refreshing in this stilted Media Age. Show tickets had already been bought so I was spared the old Lakeland custom (if it still exists) of stamping attenders at show or dance to indicate they have paid. If anyone doubts that the Lakelander lacks a sense of humour, he or she should go to Wasdale Show, where everyone is in bubbling good spirits. What matter if the first tale I heard must have been recounted when John Peel was a lad. It concerns the visitor to Wasdale Church who commented on the paucity of gravestone, remarking: "It doesn't look as if people die very often up here." The local man replied: "Nobbut yance."

Now we were in a wash of Lakeland speech, with lots of yans and gurts, the odd thrang and lig, and a single miff-maff when somebody was thought to be talking a lot o' nonsense. Greetings were shouted at a range of a hundred yards. Affability abounded. Prize herdwick tups, as white faced as clowns and with fleeces in all the glory of show-red, ground their teeth or butted each other through boredom. These noble animals were confined in pens when they would have preferred the open fell. They stood stoically, on legs like those of an oaken table, and tried to ignore all the fuss and blather around them.

When the time came for a herdwick tup to be put on show for judging, a farmer grasped its horns as he would "tak hod" of the handlebars of a bike. The herdwick had a highly-efficient braking system and, when feeling peevish, had to be slurred into position. The proud owner placed its feet so they would show off the animal at its best. Next, he was grasping a horn with one hand and fluffing up any crushed wool with the other. The men wore their colourful plastic showerproof clothing almost like a uniform and clumped about in wellies.

I was astonished at the number of bearded characters. Into view came men who might have walked straight from the pages of Thomas Hardy. I saw beards with hair as stiff as scrubbing brushes. For every tidy beard, three were as out of control as convolvulus on a wall. I suggested to one of the bearded brethren he would have to be careful at sheep-dipping time or he'd be chucked into the trough with the sheep. Joss Naylor, farmer and fell-runner, stood out among the sheepmen because he was clean-shaven. So was the stick-maker—a man with a jolly laugh—who told me he had been making crooks and sticks for forty years. I asked him what the standard shepherd's crook was made of and he replied: Ram's horn and hazel." "Where do you get the hazel?" "Off hazel bushes..." He gave another jolly laugh. When his face muscles had settled down, he said: "Hazel is ready to be gathered when t'sap's gone in."

Everyone was out-shouted by the man at the mike. He announced a race for children. When the entrants had gathered, he handicapped them, beginning with the words: "Who's got t'shortest legs? You! Have a long start. Come on..." A pause. The booming voice continued: "When I say 'go' you run like... (A pause)...You run fast! Now listen. Don't start just yet." I returned to the sheep-pens and to the multi-hued sheepmen. A farmer explained to me who was allowed to show sheep. "It goes parish by parish. 'Valley shows' will only allow stock from their own valley and perhaps the two neighbouring valleys. At Wasdale, they allow Borrowdale in cos it's only about a minute's walk over the top of there (Sty Head Gap) to Borrowdale." The "minute" was a justifiable exaggeration, unless you happen to be piloting a jet aircraft.

A hound trail was announced. Someone referred to "dogs" and was corrected with the words: "They's hoonds!" A Sabbatical hush descended on the field as the man with the drag appeared at a distant wall and waited for the signal to advance, laying the last of the aniseed-and-oil trail on the sappy grass. As he began to run towards us, a medly of "hoond" cries was heard. A tawny tide of animals swept past him and, seconds later, the animals were clambering over a wall. We heard yelps of frustration from animals which had not made a clean passage. A line of hounds swept up the fellside beyond.

Forty minutes (and ten miles) later, t'hoonds were back. At the first sighting, the line of owners and supporters who had been languishing and chatting were alert, with every nerve and musle taut. Pandemonium broke out. The supporters shouted, screamed, whistled naturally or (if they had false teeth) used metal whistles. Owners advanced, some in a curious crouching gait, staring fixedly ahead, extending the hand with the container of food to its maximum length. There was a flurry of people and hounds. I kept my eye on the nearest animal. It had run 10 miles because there was a meal of sorts as a reward. It might be hard beef, veal, venison or (especially in warm weather) fish. If any creature knows the misery of indigestion, it must be a Cumbrian trail hound. Food isn't everything. "Running is what they're trained for. But these hoonds'd hunt foxes and deer and sich like." The hound is taught from the earliest age not to touch mutton on the hoof.

One of the owners pointed to a bloody scratch on the back of a hound, which had brushed against some barbed wire. The hound was an old 'un, as trail hounds go, and would be retired at the end of the season, in three week's time. "Then you start the puppies off for the next season..." This man walked his hound twice a day, some five miles in all. "It's partial to veal...but we vary it. How would you like it, if you had rice pudding morning, noon and night. You'd get fed up of rice pudding."

The young farmers who fussed around the sheep had their visions and old men, forming clusters of pensioners, were left to their dreams of yesteryear. Two Eskdale farmers, at Wasdale Head for the day, had been retired for over a decade. One of them was wearing "real leather boots" which had been made by Freddie Ralph of Little Langdale. A man whose grazing land had taken in a good part of Burnmoor smiled when I mentioned the old-time funeral cortege, crossing from Wasdale to Eskdale, with the coffin strapped to the back of a fell pony. The animal bolted and with it went a body. The farmer remarked: "I'se read about it in a book. They nivver knew t'end of it, did they?" Another "book story"—a gory episode—was of t'Beckside Boggle down t'Miterdale Valley. "Yon boggle went to sleep on t'settee in a farmhouse. T'farmer's wife poured some hot fat over him and killed him."

I'd been intending for years to have a good crack (gossip) with Joss Naylor. I settled, on this occasion, for a five minute chat. We had the company of Jack Ellwood, a Wasdale Head farmer, who would have won the first prize if there had been a competition for the best beard on the field. Joss is still well into farming, having a sizeable flock of herdwicks. He had been fell-running three weeks before. "I was 123rd away and 24th back. It was a real bad stormy day. A lot were going down with exposure. I just ran very steady away, nothing daft..." Joss, who had celebrated his fifty-ninth birthday in February, used to run to his work, down at Sellafield, but when he went on to shift work, about eight years ago, he took to his car. "These last few years, I haven't run the races I used to do. One of my knees has no cartilage left in it."

He doesn't run professionally. It's just for fun. One of his great achievements was running to the summits of the 214 Lakeland peaks classified as "Wainwrights"—in just seven days! He was running day and night, more or less. "An odd night or two, when we'd done a Book, we stopped and had a pint of stout and some tatie pot—anything that contained a bit of nourishment. We also had a lie down, but some nights we kept running right through."

The Wasdale Show continued to run its traditional course. For once, the attention of visitors to the upper dale were not concentrated on Great Gable and its retinue of mighty fells.

White for Remembrance

I AWOKE on that early November day to find the hills crusted over with snow—several inches of snow—in an unexpected cold snap. It was Remembrance Sunday and our little walking group intended to climb Great Gable to attend a special service at a bronze plaque. Poppies and wreaths would be reverently laid on the summit of a fell which is only 51 ft short of the magical 3,000 ft. The tradition was instituted in a quiet way by the Fell and Rock Climbing Club in homage to members who had died in the wars. The Club bought the fell and subsequently gave it to The National Trust.

A blizzard had come and gone during the night. Autumnal hues in the dales contrasted with the gleam of Winter White on high ground. Ice crackled under the tyres of the car as we drove up the M.6, where several cars had spun off the road. Bob reminded me of our nocturnal dash up the motorway to observe the sunrise. We were halted by the police in a patrol car and they requested proof of the car's ownership. And would we mind telling them about our early morning mission? I gulped before saying: "We're off to watch the sunrise". Happily, they believed us. Bob had foretold that when dawn broke, a red orb would appear above the high Pennines and red light would transform the Haweswater area, with red water, red-tinted hills, red red deer and red sheep.

That morning, with cloud massing, the day did not break. Light seeped between grey cloud masses. We continued up the ridge above Riggindale and in the chilly grey light of early morning, with rain descending, we sat behind a wall—like a couple of old sheep—to make a start on our packed provisions. My fell-walking career reached its all-time low as I ate tomato sandwiches in wet weather.

Now we had to contend with ice and snow. Bob turned off the motorway for the Keswick road, which had unsalted sections. Skidding cars were performing a slow ballet without music. At Keswick, we turned on to the Borrowdale road, which (to add to the variety) was flooded in places. Derwentwater was smacking its lips against the asphalt. Grange looked like Zermatt in miniature. Further up the dale, oaks stood with arms full of colourful leaves against a backdrop of wintry fells.

Our intention was to drive to the summit of Honister Pass and use the track to the Drum House, followed by the path over the shoulder of Brandreth, to reach Gable's summit. The first Remembrance pilgrims usually set off from Honister about 7-30. This year, there would be space in which to park on Honister because hardly anyone would have been able to drive up the hill. The idea of meeting on Great Gable on Remembrance Sunday dates back to the 1939-45 war, when Alderman Glaister of Bolton decided on this novel form of commemoration. The idea was taken up by a Scout Group in Bolton. A simple, almost Quaker-like service originally had no hymns, no spoken prayers.

The hymns are still absent but a few words are spoken. One year, a friend heard the Last Post being sounded by a bugler who was out of sight, and far below the summit. A National Park Ranger musters the people at the memorial where, at eleven o' clock, the intensity of emotion is such that even the ravens seem to stop croaking. Some days are so misty, visibility is down to a few yards. It often rains but rarely snows. If a dry wind rises when the wreaths and poppies have been laid, a shimmering red cloud drifts from the felltop.

The road from Seatoller being blocked by snow, we continued along the valley to Seathwaite. There might still have been enough time to make the journey to the summit of Great

Gable by striking up the fellside by Sour Milk Gill, but instead we decided to make for the top of a fell which theoretically overlooks Great Gable from just across a valley. Great End is only sixteen feet short of 3,000 feet as compared with Gable's fifty-one. We strode to Stockley Bridge, walked into the crusty snow and slithered along the path to Sty Head, having our eyes teased by the whiteness of the high fells. Crunching snow at every footfall, we passed near Sprinkling Tarn.

The others had crampons. and walked like automata. I had only my boots and so I slithered and fell on the icefields we had to cross as we turned to begin the long drag to the summit of Great End, at the termination of the Scafell massif. The wind had produced fine snow sculptures on the ground. Bob had memories of icy grass which tinkled when it was stirred by a breeze. In the slithery conditions, we kept well clear of Great End's impressive gullies, where the Victorian climbers, wearing Norfolk jackets, Pitlochry-trousers and nailed boots had tested their skill.

Great End has been summed up by Harry Griffin as "aloof and unsmiling." It suffers (adds Harry) from being a one-sided mountain and from being just off the route to the largest peaks in England. But as a viewpoint, Great Gable is a veritable grandstand for viewing half the Lake District. We took it in turns to climb to the highest point, under an azure sky, though from round about the cairn the view was equally good. The eastward view extended to the Howgills. Westwards, low ground terminated with the Irish Sea and the main focal point was the futuristic complex of Sellafield, producer of atomic energy. The cooling towers steamed like witches' cauldrons.

Great Gable, and the depression of Windy Gap, were dotted with small black figures. At eleven o' clock we joined the Gablers in the two minutes' silence. Harry Griffin' had written of Great End as being aloof and unsmiling. He added it is easily won "and very well worth cultivating".

Winter

Ambleside has about 12—15 mornings of "snow on the ground" in the average winter. It is the same as London.

Lake District National Park booklet.

Contrary to other sheep, herdwicks are seen before a storm, especially of snow, to ascend against the coming blast...which saves them from being overblown.

Clarke, Survey of the Lakes (1787).

JOHN PEEL'S HOUSE, RUTHWAITE

FIELD SPORTS are a highly emotive issue, with a strong "anti-" element, but the John Peel tradition of fox-hunting on foot continues. (Peel, whose country lay on and around Skiddaw, was invariably seen on a pony called Dunny). The blood of Peel's hounds is represented in that of the Blencathra pack. Once the fox population was relatively small and hunt-followers spoke of a "greyhound" variety which occurred on the high fells. Now there are lots of little red foxes, some of which have been transported here from urban areas of the Midlands and North, where they are now quite common. Apart from hunting a lithesome mammal which preys on their lambs, the Lakeland sheep farmers and others enjoy a social life, for after a hunt they invariably repair to a hostelry for ale and songs from a rich oral tradition.

Swan Lake

A CHORUS of bugle-like calls—*hoop-hoop-hoop*—draws attention to a herd of whooper swans at winter quarters in the Lake District. Each October, a few family parties arrive to spend winter weeks in feeding, preening, resting—and bugling. The whooper swan loves the sound of its voice—*whoop-a, whoop-a,* with the second syllable at a higher pitch. It is a ringing call when heard in flight and somewhat subdued as the bird swims.

The largest concentration of whoopers is to be found at Caerlaverock, just north of Solway. The sky is always busy and whoopers share the airways with Bewick's and mute swans. A babbling throng of barnacle geese, which nest in Spitzbergen, crosses the sky with the noisy impatience of children being let out from school. At Caerlaverock, a visitor sees family parties of whooper swans—two Persil-white parents and their greyish young. At feeding time, when food by the barrow load is doled out, visitors watching from close range are separated from the avian throng by the plate-glass windows of a commodious hide.

Whooper swans, spilling air from their capacious wings and using their webbed feet as air brakes, plane down on Elterwater and Grasmere. I have watched a herd of swans grazing on farmland near Kirkby Thore and somewhere in my collection of transparencies is a shot of maybe sixty birds in flight, with the a haylage-tower at a farm forming part of the backdrop.

Popular romance connects the wild swans most closely with shallow, reed-edged Elterwater, which is said to be from a Norse word meaning "swan lake". This is a lake that no one really knows because access to its shores is restricted to the footpath from the village to Skelwith Bridge and, for much of the time, there are intervening trees of the ragged Lakeland "mix". The birds seen today must be the lineal descendants of those which, a thousand years ago, raised families in the lavascapes of Iceland and then flew over 500 miles of the grey wastes of the North Atlantic to winter in Britain.

A whooper is distinguishable from a mute swan by reference to its beak. Head and beak taper to a point. The base of the whooper's bill and much of the lower border of the upper mandible are yellow. And the whooper lacks the black knob which is a prominent feature of the head of the mute swan. The whooper's wings lie close to the back as it swims. Unless it is feeding, the neck is held up, straight as a broomshaft. Whoopers may have the close company of Bewick's swan, a species named after the Northumbrian engraver who specialised in birds. Bewick's swan nests much further north than the whooper, favouring the Arctic tundra, where—alas—there have been recent major oil spills.

The Rev H A Macpherson, author of *A Vertebrate Fauna of Lakeland* (1892)—a book which has been used as a quarry by a host of Lakeland students—noted the characteristics of whooper swans when he settled down to some swan-watching at Monkhill Lough. Four birds were in view. "They were feeding in company, and all four necks were sometimes straightened or bent forward at the same instant. For a few moments they would observe silence; then they 'hooped', and vociferating their peculiar clang, they all fell to feeding again. So closely did they 'herd' together that two birds might often be mistaken for one..." Macpherson contrasted "the long-drawn, flat bodies of the whoopers" with the more rounded outline of the mute swan—yet another important guide to identification. "The wild fellows swam together... Only when we showed ourselves more openly did the whoopers forego their attitude of disengaged ease." Macpherson, parson-naturalist, then disturbed dusty records going back to the seventeenth century for evidence that "the Hooper, or Whistling Swan" was a Lakelander.

Swans were among the birds consumed with gratitude by the better-off as a change from fare which had been salted down. In the following century, whoopers were reported to visit Ullswater only preceding or during severe frosts, their appearance being "looked upon as the prognostic of a hard winter." Macpherson lived at a time when many local naturalists were not discriminating between whooper and Bewick's, neither of which—in the days before special waterfowl reserves were established—allowed themselves to be viewed at close range.

Whoopers which crossed the uneasy ocean touched down on the Solway and then spread out. Many of them had to fly through gunshot. It was a time when any unusual bird was shot for further study. The local landowner had no scruples about downing a swan. In the severe winter of 1794-5, three of a flock which frequented the Esk near Netherby were shot by Sir James Graham and his gamekeeper. In 1803, the groom to the Right Hon Thomas Wallace of Carleton-hall, shot a swan on the Eamont, outflow of Ullswater. In that same year, three swans were reported to have been shot at Bassenthwaite Lake, where "upwards of 30 Swans" had been seen. In 1838, Dr Cockburn slew two swans on the Lowther river, near Bampton. Occasionally, a swan was taken live, as in the case of "a poor industrious man of the name of Musgrave", who had caught a swan and now hoped to sell it to the Lawsons of Brayton, who had a waterfowl collection. For the sake of the bruised and battered swan, I hoped he was successful.

Caerlaverock (to the north) and Martin Mere (to the south) provide safe wintering grounds for swans, geese and ducks. Everything possible is done to improve the habitat so that there is good feeding and water for bathing and to provide sanctuary. Regular feeding means that swans which are truly wild in their northern breeding grounds are in such vast numbers that some of them become quite peevish when competing for grain spread at the water's edge. On my last visit to Martin Mere, in February, there were an estimated 1,500 whoopers and Bewicks. The birds were gleamingly white against the dun colours of the land and the blue-black of a passing storm cloud. I thrilled to the almost constant bugling calls of these northern birds. As feeding time drew near, the swans began to converge on the area where the grain would be spread. The graceful swans were in the company of pochard, coot and mallard. In the distance, a flock of about 8,000 pink-footed geese took flight. Their massed voices reached me faintly, the sound merging with the conversational trumpeting notes of the swans.

I was impressed by the vast number of birds but prefer to watch the family party of whoopers on Elterwater or Grasmere. There is double beauty as their bodies are reflected in calm water. There is an operatic splendour at Grasmere in a backdrop provided by high fells.

An Aircraft on Helvellyn

A SOMEWHAT bemused Professor of Greek was the only man on Helvellyn on that breezy day, December 22, 1926, when John Leeming landed a light aircraft. The touchdown occurred at precisely 1.35 p.m., as testified in writing by Professor E R Dodds, of Birmingham University. There can have been no stranger sights on Helvellyn (3,118 ft) than that of a parked biplane, an Avro 585 Gosport which, being still at the experimental stage, had not yet been awarded a certificate of airworthiness but had been flown through severe turbulence and against a stiff easterly breeze for a touch-down on a mountain summit.

The crew of the Avro consisted of Leeming, who was chairman of the Lancashire Aero Club, and Bert Hinkler, chief test pilot for A V Roe and Company. The bid to put an aircraft down on Helvellyn had taken place in secret, a previous attempt having failed through bad weather. Now, the aircraft left Woodford at an unpromising time of the year—three days before Christmas. On the last leg of the journey, air-pockets were a worry. In one slack area, the aircraft fell like a stone for 500 ft before control was regained. The airmen had safety belts, though in turbulence Hinkler was lifted clear of his seat; and the wind took a cushion and also a letter which was to have been delivered to Mr J Sandham, Manager of the Thirlmere Waterworks.

In this bid to land on a mountain there was no back-up, as today, from a sophisticated radio system nor had the Lake District a mountain rescue service. When the Avro developed fuel blockage problems, Leeming was forced to land it in Calgarth Park, where the children of the Ethel Hedley Memorial Hospital, in a fever of anticipation about Christmas, thought that Santa Claus was about to visit them. The aircraft took to the sky and, ten minutes later, made what Leeming was to call "a splendid landing" on Helvellyn. The two men knew every inch of the ground from previous visits but did not land at either of the selected places, some distance from the summit. "We made the landing on a spot within ten yards of the heap of stones which marks the actual summit of the mountain."

The airmen chatted with Professor Dodds for twenty minutes and Hinkler clambered into the pilot's seat to be photographed. The pictures taken would give the impression it was Hinkler, not Leeming, who had piloted the aircraft. In his report, Leeming underplayed the drama of the take-off. The ridge runs north and south; the wind was blowing strongly from east to west. There were 30 yards between the plane and the rim of a 1,000 ft precipice. The pitch of the engine rose as John Leeming coaxed from it the maximum power. The aircraft "taxied" for a few yards and then the speed was increased. With a few yards left, it climbed from the mountain, circled and passed over Grasmere, paid a second visit to the children of Calgarth and then headed for Windermere, where a fuel stop had been arranged.

The Avro was then flown to its base at Woodford, near Manchester, and that evening Tom Scott, of the *Rothay Hotel*, Grasmere, had a telephone message from Leeming reporting that the mission had been successful. When the first news bulliton was broadcast from Manchester radio station that evening, Leeming briefly announced he had successfully landed and taken off from Helvellyn. His name went down in the record books as the first aviator to land on a mountain summit. He said: "The plane has behaved splendidly throughout."

The exploit was commemorated by an inscribed limestone tablet weighing one and a half hundredweight and hauled up the slopes of Helvellyn on a horse-drawn sledge. When, in 1980, British Aerospace proposed to replace the monument, planning permission was not granted. Then Michael Berry, the managing director of English Lakes Hotels, moved by the event of that winter's day, sixty years before, as recorded by Peter Connon, the chronicler of Lakes aviation history, carried out further research and made another effort to obtain the planner's permission, this time to replace one carved stone with another. His persistency paid off. Repairs to the original stone had been carried out in the 1960s but all traces of the lettering had been obliterated by the extremes of mountain weather.

A slate tablet lettered by John Gaskell, a stonemason at Keswick, was conveyed from Thirlspot on to Helvellyn on a November day, the tablet riding pillion on a motor cycle driven by Mr Gaskell, whose interests included trial cycling and, at other times, fell-walking and climbing. On the anniversary day, Michael Berry and his guests assembled on Helvellyn and at 1 p.m., the approximate time of the landing by the Avro aircraft, the new memorial was unveiled at a simple ceremony.

Michael wrote to me after the commemoration: "The weather was brilliant for us; the car park was choc-a-bloc and over a hundred people were on the summit. Two grandsons of John Leeming contacted me, one from Henley-on-Thames and one from Oxford. Both came up for the event and neither knew of the existence of the other, so there was a family reunion as well as the celebration. Much joy for all."

Felltop Ponies

WHEN I met Rufus, a fourteen-year-old fell pony, he was performing light duties at Packway, a farm near Bowness where Peggy Crossland and her sister kept some of the old Lakeland traditions alive. Peggy, who was secretary of the Fell Pony Society, ensured that they had several pure-bred animals. They were shiny black, with long manes and tails. Peggy told me that Rufus was born on the fells above Heltondale, part of the High Street range, at a time when a foal was untouched by human hands for anything up to three years, being then caught and broken in for riding or other duties to which the breed's strength and endurance were suited. Rufus had been sold to a man who used him for shepherding.

Peggy, so well informed about ponies, gently corrected me when I referred to the fell pony as a "galloway". The Galloway breed became extinct, she said though the name continued to be used for any small horse. The fell pony, bred in Lakeland for centuries, was particularly common on some of the eastern fells, sharing the grazings with sheep and red deer but spreading out so that some of them were eventually grazing the fells above Kentmere. The hamlet of Helton, which gives its name to the quiet, secluded dale above which Rufus was born, is one of a string of little settlements between Bampton and Askham, in the valley of the Lowther. The land rises in gigantic steps to the commons of Martindale and Bampton and to such splendid fells as High Street and Kidsty Pike.

The fell pony, one of the nine native breeds, attains a height of up to 14 hands. Its hardiness comes from a life spent on high grazings where the vegetation is coarse and the weather often foul. It thrives where many another breed would starve. If bred in the low country, it tends to lose its agility and hardiness. Peggy commented: "The real fell ponies have not been handled by man in their early years. Breaking them in is like trying to tame a red deer." Peggy had an awareness of the fell pony's place in Lakeland history. She told me about Kendal's former importance as a terminus for packhorses. It was estimated that over three hundred animals, in "trains", each consisting of about a score of animals, left the town each working day, some journeying into Yorkshire and others as far as London. Trains of ponies also followed the high passes of Wrynose (pass of the stallion) and Hardknott to Ravenglass.

One of the men who worked this route had a particular black stallion as the leading animal because it knew the way. The attendant rode a horse. The attendant usually contrived to stop at an inn. In due course, he would set the train off, have a few more drinks, catch up the animals before they reached the next inn, and so on...Peggy had twice ridden a pony by that route, which before the 1939-45 war had been a gravelly track, "nice to ride or walk upon". Packhorse traffic between the Lakes and Kendal declined in the closing years of the eighteenth century. A turnpike road was constructed, making wheeled traffic possible. In remoter areas, where the routes were still rough, industrialists who were exploiting the mineral riches of the district continued to use fell ponies as transport. If iron-ore was the product, a pony had two panniers and was capable of carrying sixteen stones of ore at a steady pace.

Stocky and sure-footed, of equable temperament and with strength and fortitude, the fell pony was of great help on the little farms of the fell country. At a farm recalled by Jonty Wilson, the celebrated blacksmith of Kirkby Lonsdale, a pony was called upon to carry a sixteen-stone man. It was the lot of Rufus, the fell pony first mentioned, to be used by a shepherd. Other ponies were harnessed to a light trap for the weekly journey to market or were used in ploughing. Although the Dales pony, a heavier animal, did most of the small-farm work, in haytime it was not unusual to see a fell pony drawing a mowing machine in steep meadows abutting the fell. Ponies bought by townsfolk at a fair like Brough Hill were set to work hauling tradesmen's carts or even strings of tubs in coal mines. There was once a fashion for using fell ponies on the polo field, the animal being remarkably nippy and handy in motion. Lingcropper, a famous old fell pony, was used at stud and also hauled the mail van from Penrith to Keswick and back, daily, for eleven years.

I used to visit Heltondale in winter for the pleasure of seeing fell ponies at close quarters. With sleet in the air, the animals were in shaggy winter coats. They put their backs to the wind as they fed on hay spread out to supplement their normal fare. Jonty Wilson, whose grandfather had a string of pack animals, used to say that a good fell pony "filled the eye" and had a gaity and courage that made no day too long and no task too hard. Its head was finely-chiselled, with a bright outlook, the prominent eyes being set well to the outside of the face. Other characteristics were a long neck set well back into the shoulders, a fairly short back and long hind quarters, with strong thighs and well-turned hocks. Dealers with a special knowledge of fell ponies looked for feet "shaped like a bell or a teacup"

By the 1980s, when fell ponies were no longer being left to themselves on the high fells, I would see the fields of Lowther Vale fill up with mothers and their foals, which were now about a month old. The time had arrived for the stallion to be released for mating. Grandmother Jane Noble, of Heltondale, used to relate that in her young days, grey ponies were preferred. Now the emphasis was undoubtedly on the dark tones, preferably black, and a "grun 'un" was rarely seen. A white pony was never popular among the breeders. Perhaps they felt that white represented a loss of hardiness, though a white star on the forehead or a white coronet (hoof band) was thought desirable by some.

Serjeant Noble, of High House, Butterwick, the owner of some of the best stock, told me of his family associations with Heltondale. His grandfather and father combined fell farming with the rearing of ponies, which, in the days before motorised transport, were in good demand. We spoke on a June day when the valley was belatedly in its spring garb. Rough weather had been experienced in March and April. In the fell country, there had been no spring grass until the end of May, by which time most of the ponies had dropped their foals. Of the foals, most of the fillies were being retained and the others were to be sold off at the back-end.

He spoke enthusiastically of the Fell Pony Society which, founded in 1893, had set down standards to be followed by breeders to safeguard the characteristics of the breed. An early supporter, Frank Garnett, was a veterinary surgeon of Windermere. The war years almost saw the extinction of the fell pony, the number of stallions slumping to five. As these had all been sired by a stallion called Blooming Heather, it may be safely said that that all registered fell ponies today can be traced back to that fabulous pony. The breed endured because one or two farmers kept their faith in it between the wars, when ponies were averaging only five pounds each.

The fell pony still ranges across the eastern fells and along the East Fellside, in the Eden Valley. It is a popular riding horse and, as such, is used at Lakeland's many trekking centres. Visiting a riding establishment in Ontario, Canada, I saw fell ponies used for carriage work. Bred on a farm in northern Lakeland, they were flown across the Atlantic as foals in a special compartment of the aircraft. The old Lakeland qualities of sturdiness and endurance were still evident. So was the famous fell pony's black coat, with the silvery highlights. This is, in truth, a handsome animal.

Ike's Kingdom

WHEN IKE stands at the door of Gillbrow, he has one of the fairest views in England. The farmstead of Gillbrow huddles against rising ground on the north side of Newlands Valley. He calls Newlands "a bonny unspoilt little valley." Ike Wilson was christened Isaac but the fell-folk (economical with speech) had soon clipped this to Ike. "Mebbe if things are not going well, I git worse names than that," he says. He presided over Gillbrow for almost forty years and then handed over its affairs to his son John and retired, with May his wife, to an adjacent cottage.

Ike was born—one of nine lads and lasses—in Mosedale in April, 1917. It was a cruel springtime, with snow plated by ice so that lambs were frozen to the ground. Two of his brothers, John and Harrison, stayed on the ancestral land throughout their lives. Ike went to the local school, which stood two miles away, during a time when there were thirty names on the register. Gillbrow, his home since 1955, is everything you would expect a Lakeland farm to be—relatively small, fashioned of the native stone and slate, the front whitened so that it gleams, not only in sunlight but when the clouds are low and rain is hurled at it by a wind full of spite. The fells cushion it from the effects of the prevailing wind, a southwester, but Gillbrow is exposed to the bite of the easterlies. There can be some "funny weather" in among the Lakeland fells. When snow fell one April 24, people said it would soon melt. It stayed and became waist deep in places.

From the farmyard, the eye takes in most of the 70 acres of "inland" belonging to Gillbrow and the fan-like sweep of the valley, extending to the back-end of Catbells. Also in view are some of the shapeliest of our fells—Scope End, Hindscarth,

Robinson. In contrast with the Borrowdale Volcanics which show themselves from Dale Head as a rim of jagged teeth on the southern skyline, Newlands has the softer, more rounded Skiddaw Slates. The peaks are conical, the valleys flanked by narrow ridges. Link them up, and you have a spectacular horse-shoe shaped walk, beginning with Maiden Moor and High Spy.

The Valley itself is a shallow green trough, being the Neuland of 1323, when land was newly-cleared. This period saw the draining of Husaker or Uzzicar Tarn. That curious name Uzzicar is perpetuated by the name of a farm. Around the rim of the vale are white-fronted farms and cottages, the largest cluster forming the hamlet of Littletown, known to Beatrix Potter before her Sawrey days, providing a setting for *The Tale of Mrs Tiggy-Winkle* (1905). The buildings of Newlands are linked to each other by a plethora of roads which have scarcely outgrown their old status of lanes. It is one area of Lakeland where a motorist is seriously concerned about getting lost. A road suddenly arches itself over a beck and an incautious driver hears the rasp of wing-mirror against stone. Just round a bend is a herdwick sheep, chewing roadside grass.

T'auld school, built by local folk in 1877, was closed (and became a church) in 1967. It, too, is covered with white paint which gives it a dreamy white appearance among the summer greens. Newlands is pock-marked with evidence of mining. The Goldscope (God's Gift) mine, which extends through Scope End, was the most famous of the systems worked by the Company of Mines Royal for a century from 1565. A walker towards Dale End sees traces of a watercourse and, across the beck, the zig-zag of a path. Mine entrances and heaps of unwanted rock give the upper dale a lived-in appearance.

Ike Wilson is one of the last of the old-style Lakeland farmers, in the sense that his mind is a repository of worthwhile Lakeland fact and lore. He is small and lish, his face often creased by a smile. In the dale country one expects farmers to have rasping voices, like old crows. Ike's voice is soft and melodic, frequently raised in song, sometimes in public, as at the local show—which cherishes Cumbrian traditions, and at the shepherds' meet, held in Buttermere each November. Sometimes, Ike sings at home of the doings of t'auld fox-hunters.

Ike has had the dalesman's love-hate relationship to Mr Fox. Nearly every farm has a mounted mask, with the fox set in a snarl. Ike talks of "fell foxes", contrasting them with the smaller, reddish-brown stock of the low country. He admires some of the foxly qualities, and especially its ability to survive in a cheerless environment. Yet he has seen its depredations among new-born lambs and, in t'auld days, free-range hens. In Ike's young days, foxes were few and far between. And those that survived the various hunts were inclined to twitch nervously. Now the fox is quite common. Ike believes it is at its most devilish among lambs when cubs are demanding food at a time when natural food is scarce.

Ike's busy days have been punctuated by the bleating of sheep—herdwick sheep and the comparatively modern incomer, the Swaledale (known as Swardle among the farm folk). The Wilson flock ranges across Robinson, named after an eighteenth century landowner, Richard Robinson. The sheep are "heafed", with lambs taking in a love of the natal land with their mother's milk. A Gillbrow sheep has its special markings, to distinguish it from the sheep belonging to other farmers—a red mark across the top of its back, also a black "pop" and IW burnt on the near horn. Robinson is not a particular good fell in winter, a time when the sheep have to be regularly fed.

Ike has cared for his sheep in sickness as well as health. When a yow was walking in a close circle, "sturdy" was diagnosed. This was caused by a parasite transmitted by dogs. Ike's drastic (but usually effective) method of dealing with it was a crude form of brain surgery—to crack open the skull of the sheep after establishing where the parasite was to be found and then lifting it out. The wound was then firmly bound up again. Ike says that "sturdy" declined as more and more dog-owners "wormed" their pets.

May Wilson, Ike's wife, was born and bred in Buttermere, just over the Hause from Newlands. She has been a typical Lakeland farmer's wife—quiet but industrious, capable of turning her hand to farm or domestic jobs, rearing children (in her case, four children) and living up to the Cumbrian reputation for hospitality. May's "cup of tea" turns out to be a mini-meal, with apologies that there is nothing hot. One of her great pleasures today is to exercise her two Scottish terriers, following the old field paths. John Wilson's wife, who is now esconsed in the farmhouse, was brought up in Wasdale—but a few miles away as the crow flies but several score miles as John's motor car travelled on courting nights.

Photographs of children, wedding couples and grandchildren adorn the cottage where Ike and May are theoretically in retirement but always find plenty to do. With five minutes to spare, Ike will stand at the door of his home, looking at one of the fairest views in England. He likes the sense of stillness on Christmas Day. "You can pop outside and look about and see naebody mich. It seems as if they're all in their houses oot o' t'road."

Coniston's Hollow Hills

THE OLD MAN frequently wears a bonnet and shawl of cloud. He and his retinue, known as the Coniston Fells, are old and careworn, with frost or snow in their ancient joints. From the village, in clear weather they present bold craggy faces, alternating with scree-choked gullies. A short walk to the Coppermines Valley reveals a landscape ravaged for its mineral wealth. The remains are not unattractive to those interested in how men emulated the mole and carried out widespread underground excavations, heaping up the surplus material to be consolidated by wind and weather. After moderate rain, the becks go white with fury. The birds which infuse some life into this stark landscape are dwarfed by the majesty of upjutting rocks. A raven, riding the wind, looks like a black fragment from a November bonfire. A peregrine falcon, in a dramatic swoop, almost passes notice as it collects a young rabbit from a tussock.

Coppermines? For three hundred years, miners seeking ore created a honeycomb of shafts and galleries. It is now a dangerous world, explorable only by the well-equipped and prudent, who test every yard of the way. The glint of water or an expanse of mud may cover rotting timbers, above a shaft which is a hundred feet deep. Two Windermere men who explored one of the mines in unusually favourable conditions reached a chamber of such dimensions that the roof was beyond the reach of their headlamps. Mountains of debris and rotting timber covered the floor. Scores of rusty chains hung from the darkness above. Later, they saw a stretch of floor covered by a crust of what appeared to be brown foil. It was judged to be iron-oxide. When a section was broken off, a footprint was revealed on the mud beneath!

The romantic explanation for the start of the mining was that local shepherds found outcropping veins which had been exposed by heavy rainfall. The first written records were kept by the monks of Furness Abbey. The serious recovery of copper began when the Company of Mines Royal was established in 1568 by Queen Elizabeth, whose main interest was in gold, silver and precious stones. She brought in miners from Ausgburg, Bavaria, and when traces of the aforementioned treasure were miniscule, her interest in the Company waned. The Bavarians (known to the local people as Dutchmen) found stone tools "in the Old Men's workings". Copper ore was transported to Brigham, near Keswick, by pack animal.

The incomers were defeated by the inflow of water, whereupon they adopted a horizontal approach, through adits or tunnels, driven laboriously by hand tools and wedges. Not only did such tunnels drain the workings but they were the means by which ore could be removed. As with most mining operations, the activities in Coppermines Valley were fitful. The operations ceased during the Civil War, after which the products of the copper mines were being taken by horse and cart to Coniston Hall, and later to Kirby Quay on Coniston Water, to be ferried to Nibthwaite. Horse and cart transport then moved it to Penny Bridge or Greenodd for shipment to the Swansea smelters. Early in the eighteenth century, when the '45 Jacobite uprising had created eddies in northern England, the Coniston mines were not operated for a while. They were closed again, about 1820, when the price of raw copper was not worth the effort of mining. When they re-opened in 1835, they operated briskly until yet another price-slump made the local exploitation of copper ore unprofitable.

Industrial archaeologists, the doyen of whom is Eric Holland, have charted the progress of work in this highly-mineralised area of Lakeland. By the mid-seventeenth century, the Austrian miners had excavated their way down to over 200 feet. Towards the end of the eighteenth century, the Macclesfield Copper Company were operating at around 570 feet. A waterwheel of impressive size was used to power the winch used for winding purposes and it also provided the energy for pumping out water. By the end of the nineteenth century, with an infusion of Irish labour, the workings had attained a depth of 1,230 ft. The key to success was in the pumping. So extensive did the workings become that when the pumping stopped for the last time it took three years for the Bonsor system alone to fill.

Bob and I followed a miner's trod from the village. He pointed out traces of the former railway. In 1859, the Coniston Copper Company had opened a railway to transport ore to Foxfield, on the main line of the Furness Railway Company. They, in 1862, absorbed the Coniston line into their system, running it for both goods and passengers. The path Bob and I were using led us to the Miner's Bridge, of single span, built between two high banks where the beck flows down a rock staircase with a great noise and flurry of foam. Across this bridge passed cartloads of dressed ore. Beyond lay the Coppermines Valley, a tormented scene, with a scattering of buildings, one or two renovated and the others now open to the sky. Irish Row, a terrace set on the fellside, looked tidy now that it is mainly used for holidays. The youth hostel, formerly the offices and manager's house at Tongue Brow, had been white-washed and reflected back the pale sunlight.

We had just gone undercover to examine some artefacts from the mining days when a tattoo of hail could be heard on the iron roof. The mining tradition extended from about 1620 to 1914, and involved crushers, rollers, buddles, jiggers and settling pits. What of the miners? We know little about them as individuals, except for a few brief references and a name, J Mara, with the dates 1874 and 1877, chiselled on a boulder by the Red Dell track. George Stevens, one of the last of the miners, whom I met in 1952, when he was eighty-two years of age, told me that the copper miners received on average a guinea a week and that when he began work at the mines, aged eleven, he was paid 4s. An imaginative visitor can evoke the sounds of Lakeland copper mining—the *krump* of explosives, rumble of wagons on underground tramways and, in the open air, the creaking of waterwheels.

The last spell of local mining ended in 1942, though in 1954 an attempt was made by McKechnie Bros to re-open mines at Bonsor and Paddy End. The price of copper, which was good, tumbled again. They had left the supervision of the work to Bill Shaw, and it was he who first told me about the Coniston mining and expressed his belief that a good deal of copper is left. "I have never seen it, but the old people told me this was so." Bill was born at Coniston in 1909. The village was then only half its present size and most of the men were employed in slate quarrying. The largest quarry, on the face of the Old Man, was owned by the Mandale brothers and employed about a hundred men. Quarrying ceased in the 1914-18 war, when the men were in the Forces or working at the iron ore mines of Furness.

When Bill was a lad at Coniston, no one could remember the great days of the mines but he had personal memories of the time prior to 1914 when a French company arrived intending to open up the mines in a big way. An electrolitic processing plant was built on the site of what had been the Tongue Brow workings. "We in Coniston were familiar with the sight of Count Henri de Varnie, the engineer. He was a rare person in those days—a man who could fly an aircraft. He stayed at the *Waterhead Hotel* in Coniston." Bill's father worked at the mines. His cousin, John William Shaw, was foreman. "I remember being taken to the mines and seeing this romantic French count. I also recall a chimney smoking at the smelter and dirty water flowing down the beck from the crushing mill. When the war started, Count Varnie was called up into the French air force and died when he was shot down by the Germans." The French interest in Coniston ended with the war; the machinery was dismantled and sent, of all places, to Greece.

When I first knew Bill Shaw, he had a house on Chestnut Hill at Keswick. His extensive knowledge of local mining was in danger of being lost until, in the company of E H Shackleton, the geologist, I persuaded Bill to write it up, as *Mining in the Lake Counties,* which now features in the bibliographies of most serious Lakeland books. It amused me when Bill, on being asked to do the work, said he did not know much about a certain area. Said Ernest Shackleton: "No one else will know any more than you do." And Bill Shaw had to agree that this was so.

Bob and I followed one of the mine tracks to a passage driven by t'auld men through living rock. Water percolating down the rocks formed a sort of water-curtain across the entrance. We speculated on the reason for a large covered structure and heard that it is a water treatment plant, converting fresh water into acceptable drinking water for the Coniston area. We selected a path up a bank of mine waste, with the beck seething in a V-shaped channel of its own making. Resting our backs against a well-masoned dam, we admired a mountain backdrop consisting of Brim Fell, Levers Hause, Swirl How and Kennel Crag. An unexpected gust of wind created a whirlwind on the dark tarn. A sound like the harness of a horse came from one of a party of cavers who had some chain hanging from his belt. I should have asked him about it. The party passed, with headlamps blazing, and disappeared into an area marked "Dangerous". It is possible to enter a system near Levers Water and follow it in stages back to the valley.

We moved into Boulder Valley. Here was the celebrated Pudding Stone, looking unclimbable from one side and (at the back) with ledges in plenty for any adventurous climber. Instead of climbing the Pudding Stone, we gave assistance to a rambler who had broken an ankle. The arrival of the mountain rescue Land Rover, full of rescuers, added a modernistic feature to an old and mine-weary landscape.

Wainwright's Last Resting-place

VISITING Innominate Tarn, on Haystacks, beside which were scattered the ashes of Wainwright the fell-walker, is the nearest I have come to a Cumbrian pilgrimage. Wainwright would have been somewhat embarrassed could he have known that I would use such a term. He was not a religious person, despite the grandeur of the Lakeland landscape, which has induced religious thoughts in many another. Dear Haystacks—as he once addressed it—was not always kind to him. Among the BBC film taken for a series based on his fell-walking is a sequence "shot" in wind and rain near Innominate Tarn. The sky was weeping for him!

On my most recent visit to Haystacks I did not make his favourite approach, from Buttermere, village, along the lake shore. Soaring crags give the impression that Haystacks, which some claim is a Norse name for High Rocks, stands much taller than it actually is. I approached from Ennerdale, via the old pony track of Scarth Gap. As I took to the fellside, passing between the stumps of conifers in a clear-felled area, I mourned the passing of the old Ennerdale. Beyond the stumps lay a plantation where trees of uniform age and appearance stood to attention, like soldiers on parade. My boots were sound-proofed by an accumulation of spruce needles. The call of a goldcrest—a whirring sound, like that of a fairy sewing machine—reassured me that some life remained in these alien Cumbrian Backwoods.

I broke from cover to find myself on a sun-baked hillside littered with stones which clacked and clinked at every footfall. The view had opened out. Pillar rose ponderously across the dale. Ennnerdale Water, in the lower part of the valley, and away to the west, was as blue as Stephen's ink. Before I stormed Haystacks' cliffbound rim, I looked down, down, down into the Buttermere valley, with its trilogy of lovely lakes, and across at Grasmoor, a mighty fell which had been cut down to size by cloud.

Wainwright was on my mind. A group of friends who wanted to raise a simple felltop memorial had been battling for four years with planners who now had rejected several suggested sites. I was glad when an idea to re-name Innominate Tarn, on Haystacks, after the celebrated fellwalker, was turned down, for the name Innominate means "nameless", and surely Wainwright himself would have detested the idea of messing around with the Ordnance map. But the National Park planners, though worried about any possible urbanisation of the countryside, might have allowed some modest memorial on Haystacks or perhaps Orrest Head. It was here, on a trip from Blackburn in 1930, that Wainwright found himself looking into the area which became, for him, heaven on earth.

On my climb, I preferred to think about him as I first knew him, when he was Borough Treasurer of Kendal and about to launch the first of his pictorial guides. When he was not meticulously keeping the town's books, A W's thoughts were on high and lonely places. He was a loner in his fell-top world, lost in his own thoughts, not suffering fools gladly, speaking—Quaker style—only when the spirit moved him. He might, if he felt inclined, utter a few sentences now and again. Virtually all his leisuretime had been divided between fell-wandering and preparing pages for guides which were unique in the sense there was not a line of type in any of them. He wanted them to be reproduced exactly as he drew and wrote them. One marvelled at the intricacy of his draughtsmanship and his ability to write with little variation in the size and character of the script.

In his fell-going, he was like the Lakeland fell farmer, travelling lightly, wearing everyday togs, with an old raincoat to turn the worst of the weather. He had no need for a rucksack, and pocketed his pipe and tobacco, his few provisions and the camera he used to photograph the fells so that he might later copy from them using Indian ink on white card. Wainwright did not even carry a compass. He marked the map and later copied from it in a way which would not be tolerated today without authority or payment.

When I reached the Haystacks plateau, I walked through the familiar labyrinth of rocks, knolls, tarns, cracks, crevices and coarse vegetation. An 18th century map of Lakeland published in *The Gentleman's Magazine* (1751) has the words "here eagles build" over Haystacks. The hill is not especially noted for its bird life. On the relatively dry parts, heather blooms, bees drone from flower to flower, and bilberries yield lustrous fruit for the fell-going birds to pick. The tarns, in their peaty hollows, are flanked by cotton grass and sphagnum moss.

Haystacks, viewed when there is a low-slung sun, and the north-facing crags are in deep shadow, looks cheerless—hostile, indeed. This feeling is strong in mist. At other times, the tarns wink back at the sun; the skylarks, like feathered helicopters, sing loudly. If Haystacks resembles Loughrigg from the point of view of the variety of features across its sprawling top, then it is also similar in being a relatively low vantage point for an arc of lofty fells. The romantic imagines the scattered tors are Haystacks, being like stacks of hay in a summer meadow.

Innominate Tarn, as I now saw it, was flecked with silver and stirred by a light easterly wind. Wainwright wanted his ashes to be laid here, "where the water gently laps the gravelly shore and the heather blooms and Pillar and Gable keep unfailing watch...And if you, dear reader, should get a bit of grit in your boot as you are crossing Haystacks in the years to come, please treat it with respect. It might be me."

There is a memorial in Buttermere Church. It is an inscribed piece of slate, placed on a window sill, leaving space for a vase of flowers and, in good weather, for a view through glass of those upsweeping crags—Wainwright's "wall of defending crags"—rising precipitously from Warnscale Bottom, near Buttermere.

HAYSTACKS